GLOBAL
Unemployment

GLOBAL
Unemployment
Loss of Jobs in the '90s

John Eatwell
editor

M.E. Sharpe
Armonk, New York
London, England

Copyright © 1996 by M. E. Sharpe, Inc.

Library of Congress Cataloging-in-Publication Data

Global unemployment : loss of jobs in the '90s /
John Eatwell, editor.
p. cm.
Based on papers presented at the New School Conference on
Unemployment, held at the New School for Social Research,
New York, on Dec. 8, 1993.
Includes bibliographical references and index.
ISBN 1-56324-581-7 (alk. paper).
ISBN 1-56324-582-5 (pbk. : alk. paper).
1. Unemployment—Congresses.
2. Unemployment (Economic theory—Congresses).
I. Eatwell, John.
HD5707.5.G58   1995
331.13′7—dc20   95-9023
CIP

Printed in the United States of America

The paper used in this publication meets the minimum requirements of
American National Standard for Information Sciences—
Permanence of Paper for Printed Library Materials,
ANSI Z 39.48-1984.

BM (c)   10   9   8   7   6   5   4   3   2   1
BM (p)   10   9   8   7   6   5   4   3   2   1

This book is based on papers presented at
the New School Conference on Unemployment,
which was held at
the New School for Social Research, New York,
on Thursday, December 8, 1993.

Contents

List of Tables and Figures   ix

Foreword
Jonathan Fanton   xiii

1. Unemployment on a World Scale
   John Eatwell   3

2. America's Unaccountable Admiration for
   Mrs. Thatcher's Economics
   Wynne Godley   21

3. Convergence, Technological Competition, and
   Transmission of Long-run Unemployment
   Alice H. Amsden   41

4. Free Trade, Unemployment, and Economic Policy
   Anwar M. Shaikh   59

5. Unemployment, Capital, and Unskilled Labor
   David Schwartzman   79

6. Wageless Recovery, Wageless Growth? Prospects
   for U.S. Workers in the 1990s
   David M. Gordon   87

7. Stagnation, Volatility, and the Changing Composition
   of Aggregate Demand
   Edward Nell   109

8. Full Employment and the Inflation Constraint
   Thomas I. Palley   137

9. Stimulating Global Employment Growth
   Lance Taylor   147

10. Reflections on a Sad State of Affairs
    Robert Heilbroner   173

    Bibliography   181

    Index   189

    Contributors   197

——— List of Tables and Figures ———

Tables

1.1	Unemployment in the G7, 1964–73 and 1983–92	4
1.2	Overall Productivity Growth: GDP Per Person Employed	6
1.3	Manufacturing Productivity Growth in the G7	6
1.4	Growth of Real GDP—The "Slowdown"	9
3.1	Variations in Growth Rates of Advanced Capitalist Countries Over Time, 1820–1989	44
3.2	Declining U.S. Technological Hegemony: Some Indicators	45
3.3	The Ratio of Innovations Pioneered to Innovations Infused: An Example Comparing Convergence and Divergence	51
5.1	Indexes of Real Wages and Interest Rates and of the Wage/Interest Rate Ratio, by Decades, 1900–89	81
5.2	Indexes of Average Real Wages, Average Real Prices of Investment Goods, and Their Ratio, by Decades, 1929–87	82
5.3	Private Domestic Economy: Average Annual Rates of Growth of Labor Hours, Capital, and Capital Per Labor Hour, by Decades, 1900–90	83
6.1	Impact of Stagnation on People's Well-Being	92
6.2	Components of Decline in Workers' Employment Earnings Potential	97
6.3	What Happens to Output Growth? An Exercise in Growth Accounting	103
7.1	The Golden Age and the Iron Age	111
7.2	The Economic Records of Democrats and Republicans	115
7.3	The International "Prisoners' Dilemma"	117
7.4	Selected Components of Business Investment	122
7.5	Taxes on Corporate Profits as a Proportion of Government Receipts	125
8.1	Average Rates of Unemployment in the United States	138
8.2	The Changing Measure of Full Employment in the *Economic Report of the President*	141

Figures

2.1   Manufacturing Output: Twenty-Four Years of Stop-Go   23
2.2   Unemployment Under Stop-Go   24
2.3   Inflation During Stop-Go   25
2.4   Pre-Thatcher Manufacturing Output   25
2.5   Pre-Thatcher Unemployment   26
2.6   Pre-Thatcher Inflation   27
2.7   Inflation and Money Growth Lagged Two and a Half
      Years During the (Pre-Thatcher) Seventies   28
2.8   Manufacturing Output During Thirty-Three Years   29
2.9   Unemployment   30
2.10 Money Supply Growth (Lagged Two and a Half Years)
      and Inflation: Bang Goes a Theory!   30
2.11 Manufacturing Output During Forty-Three Years   33
2.12 Unemployment   33
2.13 Growth Rate of Money Stock   35
2.14 Flow of Net Lending to Consumers As Percent of
      Disposable Income   35
2.15 Percent Change in Consumption in Successive Four-Year
      Periods   36
2.16 Household Debt as a Percent of Disposable Income   36
2.17 Flow of Net Lending to Consumers as Percent of
      Disposable Income   37
2.18 Unemployment   37
2.19 Manufacturing Investment as a Percent of GDP   39
2.20 The Current Balance of Payments (as a Percent of GDP)   39
2.21 The Current Balance of Payments, Oil and Non-Oil   40
3.1   Intra-Triad Foreign Direct Investment, 1988 and 1989   55
6.1   Workers' Employment Earnings Potential   96
6.2   Workers' Employment Earnings Potential with
      Combined Simulated "Counterfactuals"   99
7.1   Historical Growth in Labor Productivity   113
7.2   Personal Consumption Expenditures   118
7.3   FIL of Segmented Trend Through Log of Real Gross
      Private Domestic Investment—Nonresidential 1947–91   120
7.4   Net Exports   123
7.5   Federal Government Spending   127

7.6   Federal Government Purchases, Nonmilitary:
      Durables, Nondurable, Services   128
7.7   Components of Government Spending as a
      Percent of GNP   129
9.1   Effects of Productivity Growth and Demand Saturation
      on Overall Employment   151
9.2   Effects of Faster Productivity Growth when Effective
      Demand is Wage-led   154
9.3   Effects of Faster Productivity Growth when Effective
      Demand is Profit-led   155
9.4   Effect of Faster Productivity Growth on the Growth Rate
      of Potential Output in the Wage-led Case   157
9.5   Wage-cutting vs. Productivity Growth in Reducing
      Unit Labor Costs   158
9.6   A Three-gap Model   162
9.7   An Adverse External Shock in a Three-gap Model   164
9.8   A Favorable External Shock in a Three-gap Model   166
9.9   A High Employment Profit Squeeze   169

——————— Foreword ———————

I am delighted to introduce this record of the New School Conference on Unemployment—an important initiative of the Economics Department of our Graduate Faculty. I am particularly pleased that this book includes the paper given by our guest speaker at the conference, Professor Wynne Godley of the Faculty of Economics of Cambridge University. In Britain, Professor Godley is particularly well known as one of the Seven Wise Men who act as independent economic advisers to the British government. There is no doubt in anyone's mind that he achieved that position not because for more than twenty-five years he has been a persistent critic of British government policy. Rather, it is because he has been by far the most accurate forecaster of what the outcomes of policy would be—a far more disturbing attribute.

At the end of 1993, the *New York Times* reported a fall in the U.S. unemployment rate from 6.8 percent to 6.4 percent. This fall was greeted with understandable pleasure by officials, commentators, and the general public. However, we must remember that the unemployment rate today, and for most of the 1980s, is almost double what it was throughout the 1960s. In the 1960s, conventional wisdom said that high unemployment was a thing of the past. Progress in economic theory and policy making, we thought, had taught us how to manage our affairs so as to avoid permanently the high levels of unemployment endured before the Second World War.

Experience in the last twenty years has shattered that comfortable illusion. Despite the vast number of new jobs that have been created in the United States, average unemployment rates have risen. And this is true in Western Europe as well. Today, unemployment rates in the European Community are at postwar highs.

Such high unemployment represents a dual problem. There is the economic cost of wasted resources to bear. And there is also a real threat to social stability. In Europe all the economic difficulties that stem from the breakup of the old Soviet empire have been exacerbated by the high levels of unemployment in the West. Hostility to refugees, growing racism, and social fragmentation, however they originate, are all fueled by unemployment.

At home in America, while no one would pretend that the linkages are simple, there can still be no doubt that unemployment contributes to crime, to ill health, to the alienation of young people, to the despair of older people. What is most disturbing is the feeling these days that nothing much can be done about unemployment. It is becoming part of the normal landscape of our lives, as are the problems it aggravates. Unemployment, and its attendant ills, are becoming almost acceptable.

Our society must reject that position. Unemployment is not a natural disaster like a hurricane or an earthquake—something that happens to us out of the blue that society then deals with badly or well, as the case may be. Rather, unemployment is a social phenomenon. Millions of people out of work means, quite simply, that we have failed to organize our society in such a way that full employment is secured. Because it is a problem of our making, not a natural condition, there must be a solution, if only society is willing to take the steps necessary to find and implement it.

I do not have an easy remedy to recommend. Part of the task of the papers collected in this volume is to search for possible solutions. I do believe that hard choices will have to be made if our society wishes to approach full employment—the decision to try may be the hardest choice of all, certainly the most important. It is an article of faith that the choices *can* be clarified, articulated, and judged.

I am heartened by the very fact of this volume and the conference from which it springs. It asserts that social science has a responsibility to confront the real problems of human society and to assist in the search for solutions. This was the very premise on which the New School for Social Research was founded in 1919. That premise is as pertinent today as it was then. There can be no more important task than bringing the skills and insights of social sciences to bear on the blight of unemployment and to move the question to the top of our society's agenda.

Jonathan Fanton, President
New School for Social Research

GLOBAL
Unemployment

1

Unemployment on a World Scale

John Eatwell

From 1950 to 1970 all the major industrial countries enjoyed employment levels at or near full employment. This was also a time in which world trade grew more rapidly than in any equivalent period before or since, and in which productivity growth (i.e., the absorption of technological change) was faster than at any time before or since. Inflation was also low relative to later experience. This was a Golden Age of western capitalism (Marglin and Schor, 1990). Over the same period there was a sustained improvement in economic performance in almost all of the third world, maintained in large part by the steady growth of demand emanating from the industrial countries.

A distinct break occurred around 1970, with a sharp increase in trend levels of unemployment. The increase has been greatest in the major countries of the European Union, with western Germany experiencing an almost eightfold increase (from a very low base). Only Italy had a relatively low increase, but this was from what was, for the 1960s, a high base. Canada and the United States, both relatively high-unemployment countries in the 1960s, also suffered "only" 50 percent and 130 percent increases in average levels of unemployment. Japan's experience is exceptional, having very low unemployment in the 1960s and from that low base suffering only a 120 percent increase (see Table 1.1).

The economic disruption visited upon the 1970s by oil price shocks, together with the deflationary measures taken by G7 governments in reaction to the oil price rise, might be thought to be the source of the deterioration in G7 economic performance. The OECD estimated that 20 percent of the loss in OECD real income in the mid-1970s was due to the terms of trade effect of the oil price rise. The remaining 80

Table 1.1

Unemployment in the G7, 1964–73 and 1983–92

	A. 1964–73	B. 1983–92	B/A
West Germany	0.79	6.03	7.63
France	2.23	9.70	4.35
Italy	5.48	10.13	1.85
UK	2.94	9.79	3.33
USA	4.46	6.69	1.50
Canada	4.23	9.64	2.28
Japan	1.22	2.71	2.22

Source: *OECD Main Economic Indicators*.
Note: Annual standardized unemployment rates as percent of the labor force, averaged for each ten-year period.

percent of the loss was due to the concerted deflation policies that characterized the response of the western economies to the price increase. But the oil price rises of the 1970s are not an adequate explanation of sustained high unemployment. For not only had the western economies absorbed similar rises in raw material prices at the time of the Korean War without similar slowdown, but also these new high trend levels of unemployment have persisted into the 1980s and 1990s, and were not notably affected by the collapse in oil prices and other commodity prices in 1986. It is these high trend levels of unemployment that underpin the yet higher unemployment figures produced by the current "slowdown" in the G7 economies. Today, G7 unemployment cannot possibly be considered to be purely cyclical. It is a combination of a long-term trend and the cyclical factors associated with current recessions in Europe and Japan. Indeed, it may well be that the current recession is simply another step up in the long-term level of unemployment. This suggests that unemployment in the G7 today cannot be tackled by standard counter-cyclical policies. A new approach is required.

The commonality of the unemployment experience throughout the G7, outweighing the particular economic fortunes of individual countries, is especially striking. The particular circumstances of each country will, of course, affect the distribution of unemployment between them. But the common experience suggests that the causes of high unemployment are to be found in factors that affect all G7 countries in a broadly similar manner, rather than in the individual circumstances of each country. So to devise a range of policies capable of tackling the G7 increase in unemployment requires the identification of the common factors underlying that increase.

Likely candidates for a common source of increased unemployment are: *first*, the pace of labor-saving technological change; *second*, the structural changes in world trading relationships that are associated with the increasing mobility of capital and the rapid growth of third world manufactured exports, particularly from China and the Pacific Rim; *third*, changes in the international financial environment and consequential changes in the macroeconomic policies of the G7 countries, which have, in turn, impacted on the growth performance of developing countries, notably through a reduced rate of growth of world trade and low commodity prices.

The Pace of Technological Change

It has been a common view since the early nineteenth century that technological change is a threat to jobs. In the 1950s and 1960s "automation" was regarded as the key menace. In the 1970s and 1980s the impact of information technologies and electronics has often been cited as potentially job destroying.

Whatever technological changes may have done to the *composition* of employment, there is no evidence that the speed of technological change is behind the growth in unemployment throughout the G7. If it were, then there should have been an acceleration of productivity growth in the 1980s and 1990s as new techniques sharply reduced the labor input required per unit output. In fact, the reverse has occurred. There has been a sharp slowdown in productivity growth, a slowdown that has been greatest in Japan and least in the United States and the UK (in both of which productivity growth was relatively low in the earlier period). Indeed, the slowdown in productivity growth has everywhere been greater than the slowdown in the overall growth of demand, which means that the slowdown in productivity has contributed to the creation (or at least the preservation) of jobs, rather than their destruction (see Table 1.2).

In each of the G7 countries the slowdown in productivity growth has been less pronounced in manufacturing than in the economy as a whole. Insofar as the growth of demand for manufactures has also slowed, the fact that manufacturing productivity growth has been rela-

Table 1.2

Overall Productivity Growth: GDP Per Person Employed

	A. 1961–70	B. 1981–90	B/A
West Germany	4.3	1.9	0.45
France	5.0	2.0	0.40
Italy	6.2	1.9	0.31
UK	3.3	2.0	0.60
USA	1.9	1.1	0.58
Japan	9.1	3.0	0.33

Source: *European Economy*, Annual Economic Reports.

Table 1.3

Manufacturing Productivity Growth in the G7

	A. 1964-73	B. 1983-92	B/A
West Germany	4.0	2.4	0.60
France	5.3	2.6	0.49
Italy	5.1	2.6	0.51
UK	4.2	3.6	0.85
USA	3.1	2.8	0.90
Canada	4.0	2.6	0.65
Japan	9.6	5.7	0.59

Source: *OECD Main Economic Indicators.*

tively buoyant has resulted in substantial job losses in manufacturing, notably in the UK. An exception to the general trend has been manufacturing employment in Germany, which toward the end of the 1980s had resumed a (slight) rising trend, though this has been overwhelmed by the recent downturn (see Table 1.3).

The loss of jobs in manufacturing has been exacerbated by a change in the relationship between the growth of demand and the growth of jobs. In the 1960s growing demand was associated with increasing jobs. In the 1980s, growing demand has been satisfied (even more than satisfied) by productivity growth, and jobs have been lost. It is not clear to what extent the failure of manufacturing to create jobs as in the past is due to the slowdown of demand, and to what extent it is the result of a change in the relationship between the rate of growth of demand and the rate of technical progress.

Whatever might be the case, it seems likely that a higher rate of growth of demand for manufactures, although it would probably bring with it a higher rate of productivity growth too, would at least stem the loss of jobs. And there is certainly a potential for a higher growth of demand for manufactures. Even in the most advanced of the G7 countries there are substantial proportions of the population who do not have access to the number and quality of manufactured goods that their fellow citizens regard as necessary to sustain a normal standard of living.

Structural Changes in the World Economy

An issue of growing importance is whether the rise in competition from the newly industrializing countries, particularly those on the Pacific Rim, will jeopardize job creation in the traded goods sectors of the G7 countries. The possibility of securing full employment by a higher growth of domestic demand will be significantly diminished if the competitive strengths of G7 industry are overcome by the potent combination of low third world wages and ever more mobile capital.

There has been a distinct acceleration of the penetration of developing country manufactures into G7 markets. In 1968 just 1 percent of G7 domestic demand for manufactures was satisfied by imports from the third world. By 1980 developing countries' market share had risen to 2 percent; by 1988 to 3.1 percent; by 1993 to 4 percent. Developing countries manufactures now account for 10 percent of G7 manufactured imports.

Competition from the third world certainly leads to a loss of jobs in particular sectors (typically low-skill tradables), either directly, due to loss of markets, or indirectly, as innovation in response to third world competition leads to the adoption of less labor-intensive techniques, particularly low-skill-intensive techniques (Wood, 1994). But if, despite these sectoral effects, the *overall* balance of trade is unchanged, there will be no net effect on aggregate demand. Whether there is any impact on the overall relationship between aggregate demand and employment depends on the structure of demand in the economy, including demand for nontradables, and the scale of trade with third world countries, and the pace and content of technological change in the various sectors of the economy.

In fact, leaving aside the impact of the oil price rises, there has tended to be a *surplus* in the balance of trade between the G7 and the more dynamic of the third world countries; indeed, these countries are typically the fastest growing markets in the world. This was particularly true in the 1970s. Since then overall G7 trade has moved closer to general balance with this group of countries, and this deteriorating trend may well result in a G7 deficit later in the 1990s.

The impact of low wage competition from the newly industrializing countries is not dissimilar from the competition that the northern European countries experienced from southern Europe in the late 1950s. That competition, which resulted, for example, in the growth of Italy's share of world manufactured trade from less than 2 percent to over 6 percent in twenty years, did not result in unemployment in northern Europe. On the contrary, throughout the period in which competition was most intense, northern Europe suffered from a labor shortage, with about 10 percent of the labor force in West Germany and France being immigrants. The structural changes associated with the development of Italy took place in the context of generally high growth rates. The structural adjustments heralded by the rapid growth of manufactured exports from the developing countries appear threatening today because of persistent slow growth in the G7.

If in the 1990s competition from the newly industrializing countries does result in increasing deficits with the G7, then they could be dealt with (to some extent) by the traditional method of changing the exchange rate between surplus and deficit countries. The effectiveness of exchange rate changes will, of course, be limited if the penetration of G7 markets were due to the technological superiority of the imports. For example, the impact of Korean steel on the U.S. market is typically attributed to technological superiority of the product in an industry in which labor costs are a very low proportion of total costs. Whatever the character of third world competition might be, the continued growth and prosperity of the G7 rests on maintaining its technological vitality, both in the quality of research and innovation and in the quality of the labor force.

Changes in the International Financial Environment, and Their Impact on Macroeconomic Policies and Employment in the G7 Countries

The key to understanding the growth in unemployment throughout the G7 would, therefore, appear to be the third common element, the slow-

Table 1.4

Growth of Real GDP—The "Slowdown"

	A. 1964–73	B. 1983–92	B/A
West Germany	4.5	2.9	0.64
France	5.3	2.2	0.42
Italy	5.0	2.4	0.48
UK	3.3	2.3	0.69
USA	4.0	2.9	0.72
Canada	5.6	2.8	0.50
Japan	9.6	4.0	0.42
Developing countries	5.6[a]	3.7	0.66

Sources: OECD *Main Economic Indicators;* UNDO *Industry in the 1980s,* 1985; *UN World Economic Survey,* 1993.

Note: [a] 1960–70.

down in the trend rate of growth of demand (Table 1.4). This slowdown occurred around 1970, and has persisted ever since.

Real GDP growth in developing countries reveals a similar pattern. However, this similarity masks the fact that in the intervening period, developing countries' growth was sustained at a relatively high level. From 1973 to 1982, real growth in developing countries averaged 4.7 percent per year, compared with 1.9 percent in the United States, 2.4 percent in the European Community, and 3.9 percent in Japan. Moreover, aggregate figures for "developing countries" disguise significant differences in growth in different parts of the world, particularly in growth of GDP per capita. In the period 1983–92, GDP per capita fell in Latin America (at a rate of –0.1 percent per year), in Africa (–0.9 percent), in West Asia (–3.3 percent) and in the developing countries of the Mediterranean region (–1.5 percent); but grew in South and East Asia (+3.8 percent) and China (+7.9 percent).

The *persistence* of the slow growth of demand into the 1990s seems to have been predominantly caused by the change in the structure of international finance and the consequent impact on the structure of domestic macroeconomic policies. The slowdown has from time to time been attributed to a number of other factors, including the growing profit squeeze at the end of the 1960s, the exhaustion of easy opportunities for technological "catching up" with the United States, and, of course, the impact on the growth of demand of the rise in raw material prices, particularly oil prices. But none of these seems to have an explanatory power comparable with that provided by changes in international financial relationships (see Glyn, Hughes, Lipietz, and Singh, 1990).

Two fundamental institutional changes mark a clear break in the international environment: first, the collapse of the Bretton Woods fixed exchange rate in the early 1970s resulted in the 1970s and 1980s being an era of floating rates; second, the regulated financial markets of the 1960s were replaced by the deregulated global markets of the 1980s.

There has been extensive analysis of the inability of the post–Bretton Woods trading and payments system to deal with international trading imbalances other than by deflation and growing unemployment in weaker countries—a deflationary impulse that has proved contagious. Less attention has been paid to the fact that this deflationary pressure is reinforced by the deregulation of global markets and the huge growth in short-term capital flows.

Financial markets are today dominated by short-term flows that seek to profit from changes in asset prices—in other words, from speculation. The growth in the scale of speculation, relative to other transactions, has been particularly marked in the foreign exchange markets over the past twenty years. It is estimated that in 1971, just before the collapse of the Bretton Woods fixed-exchange-rate system, about 90 percent of all foreign exchange transactions were for the finance of trade and long-term investment, and only about 10 percent were speculative. Today, those percentages are reversed, with well over 90 percent of all transactions being speculative. Daily speculative flows now regularly exceed the combined foreign exchange reserves of all the G7 governments.

The explosive growth of short-term speculative flows originated in a powerful combination of the carrot of profit and the stick of financial risk.

To an important extent, speculation is an inevitable outcome of the abandonment of fixed rates. Under the Bretton Woods system there was little profit to be had in speculation, since currencies moved only in very tight bands, apart, that is, from the very occasional change in parity. Indeed, the Bretton Woods system provided quite remarkable stability. For example, the core currencies of the European Monetary System, locked together in the 1980s in the Exchange Rate Mechanism (ERM), enjoyed *greater* stability in relation to one another during the

Bretton Woods era than they have been able to achieve since. In the face of Bretton Woods stability, it was not worthwhile maintaining the large-scale currency dealing facilities with which we are familiar today—even if the contemporary regulatory structures had not placed significant barriers in the path of short-term capital flows.

However, once Bretton Woods had collapsed, and significant fluctuations became commonplace, then opportunities for profit proliferated, regulatory structures that inhibit flows of capital were challenged as "inefficient" and "against the national interest," and the infrastructure of speculation was constructed. The Bretton Woods system was finally abandoned in 1973. The United States announced the elimination of all capital controls in January 1974.

The incentive to deregulate international capital flows, which was created by the abandonment of fixed rates, was decisively reinforced by the need to hedge against the costs that fluctuating exchange rates imposed on the private sector. Under the Bretton Woods system, foreign exchange risk was borne by the public sector. With that system's collapse, foreign exchange risk was privatized.

This privatization of risk imposed substantial strains on the domestic and international banking systems. The need to absorb and cover foreign exchange risk demanded the creation of new financial instruments, which in turn required the removal of many of the regulatory barriers that limited the possibilities of laying off risk, and a restructuring of financial institutions.

Combined with other, domestic, pressures for the removal of financial controls, the collapse of Bretton Woods was a significant factor driving the worldwide deregulation of financial systems. Exchange controls were abolished. Domestic restrictions on cross-market access for financial institutions were scrapped. Quantitative controls on the growth of credit were eliminated, and monetary policy was now conducted predominantly through management of short-term interest rates. A global market in monetary instruments was created.

Today the sheer scale of speculative flows can easily overwhelm any government's foreign exchange reserves. The ease of moving money from one currency to another, together with the ease of borrowing for speculative purposes, means that enormous sums can be shifted across the exchanges—especially for short periods of time. Prior to the September 1992 run on sterling, the British government boasted of a $15 billion support facility it had negotiated in Dmarks, to be used to defend the parity of the pound. Yet, when the speculative storm broke, that sum would be matched by the sales of sterling by just one prominent player in the foreign exchange markets.

The overwhelming scale of such potential flows means that governments must today, as never before, keep a careful eye on the need to maintain market "credibility."

Credibility has become the keystone of policy making in the nineties. A credible government is a government that pursues a policy that is "market friendly"; that is, a policy that is in accordance with what the markets believe to be "sound." Particularly favored are measures designed to meet a "prudent" predetermined monetary target, such as maintaining a given exchange rate parity, or a given growth rate of the money supply. Governments that fail to pursue sound and prudent policies are forced to pay a premium on the interest costs of financing their programs. Severe loss of credibility will lead to a financial crisis.

The determination of what is credible, and how governments lose credibility, is a product of the way that speculative markets actually work.

In his *General Theory*, John Maynard Keynes likened the operations of a speculative market to a beauty contest. He was not referring to a 1930s equivalent of the Miss World contest. He had in mind a competition that was then popular in the British tabloid Sunday newspapers in which readers were asked to rank pictures of young women in the order that they believed they would be ranked by a "celebrity panel." So in order to win, the player should express not his or her own preferences, but the preferences he or she believed were held by the panel. In the same way, the key to playing the markets is not what the individual investor considers to be the virtues or otherwise of any particular policy, but what he or she believes everyone else in the market will think.

Since the markets are driven by average opinion about what average opinion will be, an enormous premium is placed on any information or signals that might provide a guide to the swings in average opinion and as to how average opinion will react to changing events. These signals have to be simple and clear-cut. Sophisticated interpretations of the economic data would not provide a clear lead. So the money markets and foreign exchange markets become dominated by simple slogans— larger fiscal deficits lead to higher interest rates, an increased money supply results in higher inflation, public expenditure bad, private expenditure good—even when those slogans are persistently refuted by events. To these simplistic rules of the game there is added a demand for governments to publish their own financial targets, to show that their policy is couched within a firm financial framework. The main purpose of insisting on this government "transparency" and a commitment to financial targeting is to aid average opinion in guessing how average opinion will expect the government to respond to changing economic circumstances, and how average opinion will react when the government fails to meet its goals.

The demands of credibility have imposed broadly deflationary macroeconomic strategies on the G7. In the 1960s, the managed international financial framework permitted expansionary, full employment policies that were contagious both domestically, encouraging private investment, and internationally, underwriting the growth of world trade. In the 1980s, the deregulated financial framework has encouraged policies that elevate financial stability above employment. This has ratcheted up real interest rates, which have in turn reduced domestic investment and slowed the growth of world trade.

Financial instability has a severe impact on the ability of companies to invest with confidence, and, indeed, on their ability to survive. The globalization of financial markets has meant that whereas international disequilibria may, in the past, have been manifest in exchange rate movements, today they have an impact on interest rates in domestic money markets. The instability of local interest rates means that international financial pressures are felt by small and medium-sized firms operating in the home market, and not only by large companies operating internationally.

These new pressures on small firms have major implications for any drive to create new jobs. Between 1979 and 1991, employment in the Fortune 500 companies in the United States fell from 16.2 million to 12 million. By contrast, the Bureau of Labor Statistics estimates that of the net total of 18.5 million jobs that were created in the 1980s, 12 million were created by new, mainly small, companies. Small and medium-sized firms are the job engines of the G7, and it is these firms that are most severely hit by financial instability transmitted through the global money markets.

Instability has a further negative effect on policy. It severely reduces the scope of the fiscal cooperation that G7 countries so desperately need to engineer a concerted attack on unemployment. With exchange rates fluctuating, the distribution of the gains of such a concerted strategy is highly uncertain. But if the "payoff" is unknown, it is difficult for governments to commit themselves to cooperative strategy, particularly when that strategy carries the risk of loss of credibility.

A Full Employment Strategy for the G7?

The Golden Age of full employment was a product of a particular combination of international relationships—a combination that collapsed in the early 1970s. Much of the rise in G7 unemployment since then can, I believe, be attributed to that collapse. If this argument is correct, then the pursuit of a full employment policy must involve *either* withdrawing from the international pressures that create unemployment (the "war" or "siege" economy solution) *or* the creation of an international environment that replicates the expansionary framework of Bretton Woods.

Simply to pose the issue indicates the scale of the task. However, there is no intrinsic reason the G7 should not be able to create a new international regime that would underwrite national full employment policies.

"Back to Bretton Woods" is not a feasible proposition. The Bretton Woods system rested on the economic dominance of the United States. That economic dominance produced a worldwide desire for dollar reserves and the consequent ability to fund international imbalances by flows of United States capital. Bretton Woods was not a multilateral system. It was United States–led, and was therefore incapable of dealing with the imbalances caused by the relative economic decline of the United States itself.

Neither of the two other dominant economies in the G7, Germany and Japan, occupies a position comparable to that occupied by the United States in the immediate postwar period. Leaving aside the temporary impact of reunification, Germany has run a large and persistent current account surplus for the past thirty years. But long-term capital flows out of Germany have never been sufficient to fund the counterpart deficits in other countries in the way that United States capital flows did in comparable circumstances. As far as Japan is concerned, the yen has not achieved the role in international trade played by the dollar even today, especially in third-party transactions. While Japanese exports amount to 16 percent of total G7 exports, only 7.5 percent of G7 exports are invoiced in yen. By contrast, 42 percent of G7 exports are invoiced in dollars, even though the United States is the source of only 21 percent of those exports.

So a new Bretton Woods must be a genuine multilateral arrangement, forged out of the current G7, dominated by the leaders of the world's three main currency blocks: Germany, Japan, and the United States. At the core of that new system should be a renewed commitment to securing the currency stability that is necessary to underwrite the coordinated international expansion needed to avert worldwide recession. The present largely ceremonial summits of the G7 would need to be replaced with meetings that actually deal with substantive issues. A permanent secretariat should be created with the skills and authority to manage the international payments system.

It is often argued that a new stable currency system is simply not feasible in a world of deregulated finance linked by the modern technology of the money markets. This argument fails to take into account the fact that fluctuating rates are themselves the motive force behind the very existence of large-scale speculative infrastructure. Moreover, while the speculators may be able to borrow very large sums for short periods of time, the central banks, as the creators of currencies, can, collectively, provide indefinitely large sums for just as long. New cooperation between the major central banks and the creation of new techniques of domestic monetary control (and "sterilization") are vital if stability is to be restored.

It will not, of course, be possible to create a new stable system if there are persistent trade imbalances in the G7 that are not funded by long-term capital flows. Today, the fundamental imbalance is between the United States and Japan. European Community trade is broadly balanced—and has been for more than the past decade. The yen losses suffered on Japanese financial investments in the United States, combined with current difficulties in the Japanese financial sector, suggest that financing a persistent U.S. deficit is going to prove more difficult in the 1990s than it did in the 1980s. Sustained growth and expanding trade will therefore require action to correct the trade imbalance between the United States and Japan. The alternative is either persistent instability, or the stability of permanent recession.

A G7 agreement to buttress economic policy coordination with a framework of stable exchange rates must be reinforced by action to monitor and perhaps regulate short-term international capital flows.

Attempting to maintain stability in international currency markets under the current deregulated regime is like trying to cross an uneven field carrying a large volume of water in a shallow pan. It would be much easier if the pan contained a number of baffles to prevent all the water from slopping in unison from side to side. Financial baffles are needed to slow down the rush of short-term capital from one currency to another.

The technical problems involved in creating suitable baffles in the international financial markets are typically overrated. The fact that trading today is typically by electronic transfer makes effective monitoring easier than ever before, and, with international agreement, it would not be too difficult to link the legal right to trade to the requirement to accept appropriate monitoring. Effective monitoring is the starting point of effective management. Both will be possible only if there is full and consistent cooperation among the G7 countries, in the pursuit of agreed objectives.

A Full Employment Strategy for the European Union

The European Union forms what is virtually a closed economy. The proportion of foreign trade in EU GDP is slightly lower than the proportion of foreign trade in the GDP of either the United States or Japan. Moreover, the EU external account is typically in balance and much more stable that the current account balances of either the United States or Japan, or indeed the member states.

This suggests that there is considerable potential for the EU to pursue a "domestic" full employment strategy, whatever happens in the rest of the G7. Unfortunately, the EU does not possess the institutions capable of pursuing such a strategy: monetary coordination is highly imperfect, and insofar as it exists at all is dominated by the domestic concerns of the Bundesbank; fiscal coordination is nonexistent.

It is difficult to envisage effective policy coordination in the near future. The current exchange-rate regime, in which several currencies, notably the pound, are floating against the Dmark, means that estimation of the national payoff from any coordinated fiscal expansion is virtually impossible. Any country that devalued during the expansion would "steal" jobs from the others. An exchange-rate regime that, by its very nature, creates an environment in which member states *compete* over the allocation of employment between them is hardly conducive to fiscal policy coordination.

Moreover, the persistent EU external balance is a less secure foundation for coordinated fiscal expansion than might at first be supposed. The overall external balance is the result of netting out third-party transactions. But in the coordinated expansion, the relationships with third parties will contribute to the pattern of surpluses and deficits. The UK, for example, might maintain a balance with EU partners but suffer a severe deficit with non-EU countries, the counterpart of which might be a German surplus with non-EU countries. The EU as a whole would stay in balance, but the UK deficit might then force abandonment of its part of the growth strategy, bringing down the entire, interdependent effort. So policy coordination is made difficult within the EU, simply because member states have substantial trading relationships with economies that are not part of the coordination process, and the surpluses of one member state are not available to fund the deficits of another.

These factors are just some of the difficulties involved in creating an effective coordinated fiscal expansion (see Eatwell, 1994a, 1994b). Yet given the high level of interdependence that has developed between the EU economies (about one in five of all jobs in the UK are directly dependent on demand from other EU economies), some structure of institutions that permits coordination, of monetary *and* fiscal policies, must be devised if the EU is not to suffer permanently high levels of unemployment.

This will require the creation of an entirely new institutional framework, not previously encountered in the history of modern capitalism. The Bretton Woods era was not a period of policy coordination. The fixed-exchange-rate system was buttressed by strict capital controls and by active trade policies, against which the dominant economic power, the United States, did not retaliate. (For a full account of the trade policies of this era, particularly the "management" of trade by Germany, France, and Japan, and the response of the United States, see Shonfield, 1965.) Individual countries were therefore able, within bounds, to pursue national economic objectives. That these added up to a reasonable coherent set of international growth rates is to a substantial degree attributable to the combination of managed trade and a persistent U.S. deficit on combined current and long-term capital accounts that sustained the growth of world demand. The sustained high levels of employment were the outcome of the resultant structure of national policies: interdependent, yes; coordinated, no.

A similar reliance on national policies was the basis of the recovery from the recession of the 1930s. The recovery heralded by abandonment of the gold standard, and the successive devaluation of currencies against gold, was not due so much to the devaluations (after all, it was not possible for all countries to devalue against each other, and the countries that did not devalue were not big enough relative to the world economy to act as deficit-absorbing engines of world demand). It was instead due to the adoption of national expansionary policies—notably, cheap money policies, fortified by capital and trade controls—once the need to maintain the monetary orthodoxy of the gold standard had been abandoned (Temin, 1989; Kitson and Michie, 1994).

These issues were not addressed in the Maastricht Treaty at all. The treaty embodies the implicit assumption that monetary stability is all that is required for full employment to be restored.

UK Policies for Full Employment

The international dimensions of the unemployment problem in the 1990s do not rule out unilateral action by the UK, even within the structure of the current trading and financial system. Quite simply, that will involve improving the competitive position of the UK so that more demand stays at home and more demand is attracted from abroad. In the medium term superior competitiveness will be necessary to ward off any jobs threat from the newly industrializing countries.

The economic state of Britain today is historically unprecedented. Never in modern times has Britain faced a situation in which unemployment is due to an inability to produce enough of the goods that people want to buy. In the past, even in the 1930s, an increase in demand, as a result of increased spending either by the government or by the private sector, would result in jobs being created predominantly in Britain.

That is not the situation today. Any expansion of demand today will lead to a rapid growth in imports, that is, an export of jobs. This would not matter were there increased exports to match the growing imports, provide jobs in the export industries, and create a firm base for expanding jobs in other sectors, too. Sadly, that is not the case. The economy simply does not have enough competitive capacity to produce the goods for the home market and for exports that would allow Britain to sustain a full employment level of demand, or anything like it. If there were full employment, the volume of imports would be so great, the borrowing to pay for them so enormous, that the economy would soon be crushed under the weight of unmanageable foreign debts.

That is the core of Britain's employment problem: not enough competitive capacity. And most important of all, not enough people with the skills to compete in the modern global economy, and the opportunity to use those skills with the latest techniques, producing the latest products. It is skills that really matter today. In a global economy where techniques and capital are more mobile than ever, and markets are truly international, what distinguishes a national economy are the skills and talents of its people. If those skills and talents—from management techniques to handicrafts, to computer sciences, to electrical engineering, to design—are neglected, a country first loses its competitive edge, and then slips into a decline characterized by a growing trend in unemployment.

If this analysis is correct, the attack on the problem of unemployment will require a significant rebalancing of the UK economy, with an increased share of total resources being devoted to investment in capacity, in people, in research, and in other aspects of competitiveness, including design. This poses a number of major problems for economic policy.

Private-sector investment will increase to the extent required only if there is a prospect of sales and profit, that is, if there is expanding demand. There is, therefore, a chicken-and-egg problem: the ability to sustain a higher growth of demand requires competitive capacity, investment in competitive capacity requires a high growth of demand. It is likely, therefore, that the necessary rebalancing will require the public sector to play a role, taking the intertemporal risk that the private sector is not capable of carrying, perhaps in some innovative public- and private-sector partnerships.

Rebalancing the economy also means that consumption grows more slowly than output as a whole. Recent tax increases are designed to achieve this goal. If the reduction in consumption were to be accompanied by increased investment, there would be considerable pressure on money wages to restore real income lost in higher taxes.

Part of the process of rebalancing might be aided by a more aggressive exchange-rate policy. But this is not a substitute for an investment strategy. Everything else being equal, too high an exchange rate will make British goods uncompetitive at home and abroad. Equally, even if products are old-fashioned and techniques out of date, a massive devaluation may lead to some sales. There is, after all, a market for the very cheap Russian-built Lada cars. But unless British industry is competitive, and competitiveness is maintained over time, then no level of the exchange rate is sustainable in the medium to long run. The pound has been continuously devalued against the Dmark for the past thirty years, with no obvious improvement in Britain's relative economic strength vis-à-vis Germany. Of course, it may be argued that Britain would be a lot worse off if the pound had not been devalued (going back to the 11 Dmark pound of the early 1960s would result in an export collapse). But that is to miss the point. The failure to invest, to train, to innovate on anything like the scale of Germany has not been disguised or overcome by devaluation. An economic policy that relies on continuous devaluation alone to overcome structural deficiencies is a sticking-plaster policy, incapable of tackling the real problem of productive capacity and therefore incapable of sustaining full employment.

Conclusions

The problem of international unemployment is rooted in developments in the international trading and financial system since 1973. The pressure to liberalize goods markets and, most important, financial markets, has created a deflationary climate in the G7, which has infected the wider world economy. Within this deflationary climate not only is it difficult to implement the structural reforms required in the weaker developed countries, such as the UK, but also the welcome development of formerly backward economies, such as South Korea, Taiwan, and China, is seen as a threat and an excuse for yet further deflation and deregulation.

The theory of international economic policy, the policies that emanate from that theory, and the institutions that implement the policies are all constructed around the model of a self-adjusting market system. The history of the international economy lends no support to this model. On the contrary, a sustained revival of international economy, and the attainment of higher levels of employment, let alone the attainment of full employment, requires the replacement of that model of self-adjustment with an analysis that recognizes the need for institutions to be constructed that can ensure that the growth of world effective demand is sustained and expansion, rather than deflation, becomes contagious.

2

America's Unaccountable Admiration for Mrs. Thatcher's Economics

Wynne Godley

I think it is true to say that most people, in the United States and elsewhere, insofar as they think about postwar Britain at all, think that the first thirty years or so after the war was the period when the country lost all the appearance and reality of being a great power; that this was related in an important way to the very poor performance of her economy; and that this in turn was related to such things as the class system, the power of the trade unions, the laziness of the British worker, and the amateurish attitude of British management. And Britain's decline was sped on its way by a very incompetent attempt on the part of the government to *manage* the economy with a view to maintaining full employment and steady growth without inflation. In fact, people think, these active policies only succeeding in *creating* or *accentuating* business cycles. Hence, the nickname "Stop-Go" applied to the policies of the period. And to the extent that full employment was maintained, this was at the expense of accelerating inflation. These demand management policies (it is held) were particularly dangerous because they were accompanied by policies that featherbedded lame ducks in the form of weak corporations and workers who didn't want to work, and that provided free health and education services for everyone. This was well meaning, perhaps, but deeply misguided. Then Mrs. Thatcher came along and gave the whole place a jolly good shaking up. And whatever it was exactly that she did and how exactly she did it, there was something heroic and absolutely marvelous about it all. It was just what Britain needed. And whatever clever people may say, things are in some fundamental way better now. I have sometimes had cause to recall the lines of Rudyard Kipling:

> England's on the anvil! Heavy are the blows!
> (But the work will be a marvel when it's done)
> Little bits of Kingdoms cannot stand against their foes.
> England's being hammered, hammered, hammered into one!
>
> There shall be one people—it shall serve one Lord—
> (Neither priest nor baron shall escape!)
> It shall have one speech and law, soul and strength and sword.
> England's being hammered, hammered, hammered into shape!

Kipling was, of course, writing about the years following 1066.

I am going to take the reader on a personal journey and describe—and up to a point display—what it meant to me to be shaken up by Mrs. Thatcher. By this, I don't mean shaken up in my private life and career, although there was some of that, too. I mean shaken and shocked in my capacity as a professional applied macroeconomist.

Too many people express opinions about the Thatcher period—on both sides—without backing up what they say with facts. On top of that, there has been a very determined and successful attempt to pollute the sources of information. I am going to try to convey *hard information*.

Let me start by admitting that many mistakes were indeed made by those responsible for economic policy during the first quarter century after the war. The first chart, Figure 2.1, shows the history of manufacturing output up to 1974. (The first vertical line indicates the date on which I joined the Treasury, the second vertical line the date on which I left.)

As you can see, the growth of output was, indeed, very uneven, each chancellor of the exchequer being associated with his "stop" or "go." In the early 1950s there was the Butler "go"; in 1957 there was the Thorneycroft "stop"; in 1959 there was the Heathcote Amory "go" followed by the Selwyn Lloyd "stop" in 1962. This last event made a great impression on me at the time. Selwyn Lloyd didn't mean his stop to be a stop at all. He had been briefed by the Treasury, which indirectly meant me, as I had a big role at the time in forecasting that the economy was going to expand and unemployment fall. When it didn't do so, there were bellows of fury from all informed opinion (notably two young financial journalists called Nigel Lawson and Samuel

Figure 2.1 **Manufacturing Output: Twenty-Four Years of Stop-Go**

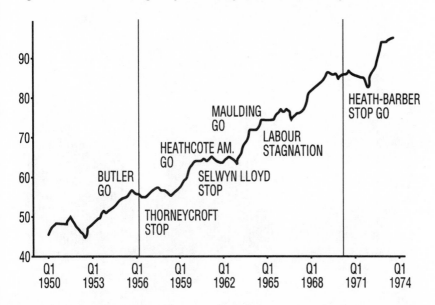

Brittan), and the wrath of the prime minister was called down on the chancellor. Although it was we who had made the mistake, it was poor Selwyn Lloyd who got the sack.

Selwyn was replaced by Mr. Maudling, who, after a decent interval of a month or two, generated another go phase, but one that was too late to save the Tories from the consequences of scandal, and disillusionment with their incompetent economic management, in the general election of 1964. The Labour government tried to keep things going but found itself compelled to apply the brakes in stages. We finish this period with the most sensational of all the go periods, presided over by the new prime minister, Mr. Heath, and his chancellor, Mr. Barber.

Figure 2.2 shows the consequences of all this for unemployment. The instability in the growth of production has a very precise counterpart in the fluctuations in unemployment. All these fluctuations were big news at the time, which, as I have already mentioned, would make or break political careers. In 1962, for example, unemployment rose to (what was then) a postwar high. This rise, the one that cost Selwyn Lloyd his job, was *to* half a million, 2 percent of the labor force. Note, too, that the *average* level of unemployment over the whole twenty-three years shown was only 2 percent.

Figure 2.2 **Unemployment Under Stop-Go**

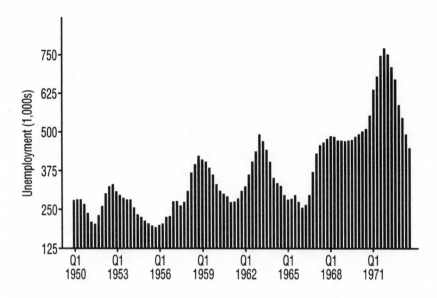

As far as inflation is concerned, as is shown in Figure 2.3, the rate of inflation, which had been at about 10 percent in the early 1950s, fell throughout the decade and actually touched zero in 1959. It is interesting, in the light of currently fashionable theories of inflation, that this decline to zero took place notwithstanding that this was the heyday of corporatism and notwithstanding that unemployment was below 2 percent for the whole of the 1950s, below 1 percent for a considerable part of the time. Note, too, that although inflation was relatively high at the end of the period, there is *no clear upward trend* as so many people believe.

A far more distressing time followed the collapse of the growth experiment sponsored by Mr. Heath—an experiment that immediately came to be regarded as the most serious error made in the whole postwar period up to that time. The consequences were inherited by the third postwar Labour administration, which lasted from 1974 to 1979.

Under Labour there was a period of stagnation different in kind from anything that had gone before. The dismal performance of output (Figure 2.4) had a very obvious and very distressing counterpart in unemployment, which rose to well over 1 million (4 percent) and stayed there (Figure 2.5).

Figure 2.3 **Inflation During Stop-Go**

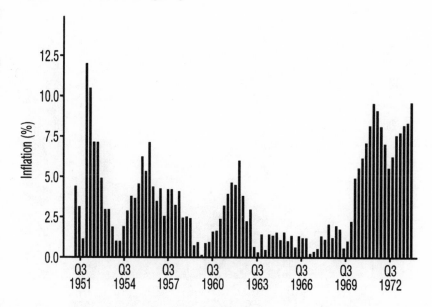

Figure 2.4 **Pre-Thatcher Manufacturing Output**

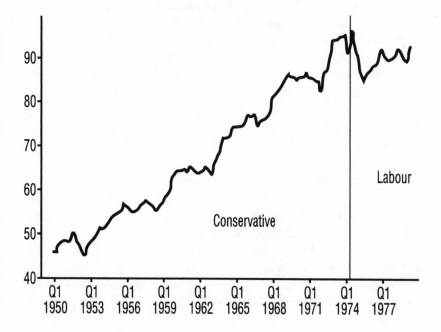

Figure 2.5 **Pre-Thatcher Unemployment**

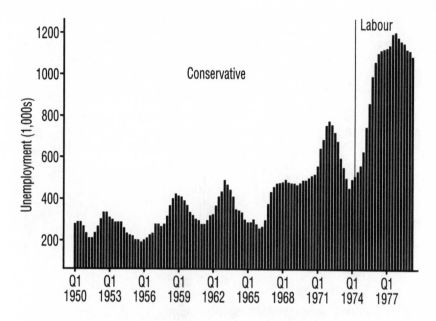

The unprecedented stagnation was notoriously accompanied by an explosion in inflation (Figure 2.6), which at one stage in 1975 reached 25 percent.

I do not believe that the inflation can be laid at Labour's door. The inflation was caused by the rise in oil and commodity prices in conjunction with the Conservatives' unfortunate wage-threshold scheme, which gave everybody a wage increase month by month and point by point for price increases above a certain low threshold. It was a most unfortunate accident that the threshold scheme was introduced just before the oil price explosion.

However, so far as output and unemployment go, I do declare the Labour government guilty. They were scared by the balance of payments deficit (largely caused by oil prices), and by a fall in the exchange rate, into deflating the economy in a way that was *not* necessary. It was just then that North Sea Oil was coming into production and the balance of payments was actually heading for *surplus*.

This failure of Labour's economic policy was the occasion for a real revolution in economic thought, which was one of the most important reasons Mrs. Thatcher came to power in the spring of 1979, and which

Figure 2.6 **Pre-Thatcher Inflation**

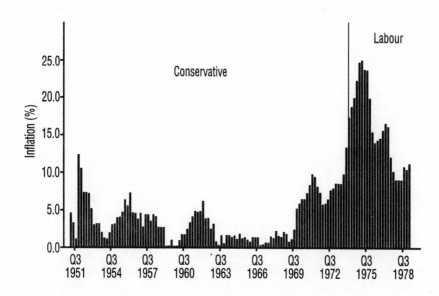

created a hopefulness about the marvelous things that were now going to be brought about. The period from about 1974 until the early 1980s was the true heyday of strict monetarism of the Milton Friedman variety. Milton Friedman has said that fluctuations in the money supply would quite inevitably lead to fluctuations in the price level of similar magnitude after a period of two years—perhaps a little more, perhaps a little less. Figure 2.7, which displays the inflation rate together with the rate of growth in the money stock lagged by 2.5 years, shows that Friedman had been proved right! The only politically correct thing to say, already at that time, was that the inflation of 1974–75 had been caused by the monetary incontinence of 1972–73.

At least equally important was the treatment of the high level of unemployment. According to the monetarist view that was now taking root, governments *could not*, by use of macroeconomic policy, change the level of unemployment, except very temporarily. Attempts to reduce unemployment by macroeconomic policy would actually be counterproductive, eventually raising unemployment above what it otherwise would have been. And this, indeed, explained why unemployment had risen in the way it had.

This initial Thatcher view of macroeconomic policy meant that the

Figure 2.7 **Inflation and Money Growth Lagged Two and a Half Years During the (Pre-Thatcher) Seventies**

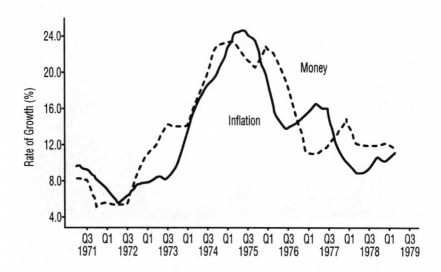

proper role of governments was simply to create the conditions under which enterprise would flourish. This required a stable, noninflationary environment. Control of the money supply, so that it stayed within well-defined target ranges, was a necessary and sufficient condition for the control of inflation. Indeed, it is quite clear from those issues of the annual *Financial Statement and Budget Report* that were published early in the Thatcher period that she saw control of the money supply as literally the only macroeconomic task that a government could properly undertake. Growth and full employment were to come as a result of the creation of a stable environment. It was essential to make market forces work better by removing rigidities in the labor market (i.e., trade union power) and by creating incentives that would make hard work and enterprise more rewarding, perhaps by reducing marginal direct tax rates.

Mrs. Thatcher and her supporters really did believe that growth and full employment would be created in this way. The disgrace of the unemployment that had risen so much under Labour was a major feature of the Conservative election campaign that brought Mrs. Thatcher to power, encapsulated in the slogan displayed on hoardings throughout the country: LABOUR ISN'T WORKING.

Figure 2.8 **Manufacturing Output During Thirty-Three Years**

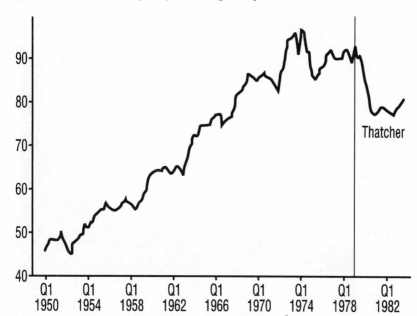

The next three figures show what actually happened in the new era of macroeconomic stability.

What was supposed to be a new era of growth and stability turned out to be the occasion for a recession enormously more serious than anything that had happened before. As is shown in Figure 2.8, manufacturing output fell by 17 percent in eighteen months. Unemployment rose to once unthinkable levels—to nearly three times what it had been under Labour and six times the level over which we agonized so in 1962, and which lost Mr. Selwyn Lloyd his job (see Figure 2.9).

Figure 2.10 shows what happened to inflation and the money supply. As in Figure 2.7, the money supply figures are lagged 2.5 years. So the money supply growth shown as relevant for the early Thatcher years is in fact that which actually took place in the last two years of the Labour government. The figure shows that Friedman's "scientific" hypothesis about the relationship between inflation and the money supply broke down the first time any government really tried to use it. As a matter of fact, it went completely wrong in three entirely different ways.

First, there was a big acceleration of inflation, although the money

Figure 2.9 **Unemployment** (1950–82)

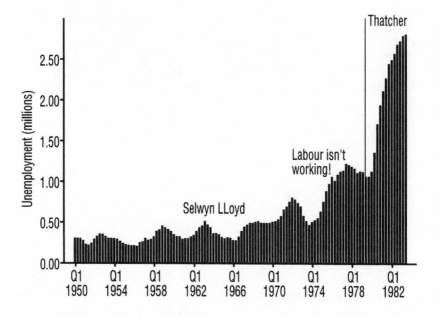

Figure 2.10 **Money Supply Growth (Lagged Two and a Half Years) and Inflation: Bang Goes a Theory!**

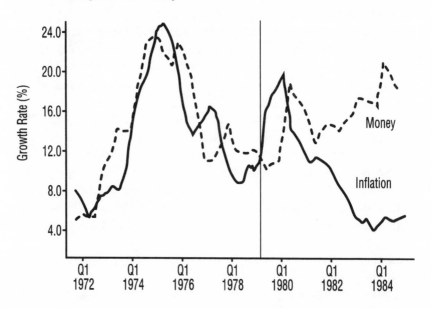

supply growth had not accelerated at all 2.5 years previously.

Second, the money supply was not under control at all, although desperate attempts were made by means of interest-rate policy. Control of the money supply was the one thing that the government claimed it would and should have, yet every target (except one) was missed, usually by a very large margin.

Third, notwithstanding the fact that the growth of the stock of money accelerated sharply, inflation *did* come down. This was the thing Friedman's scientific theory said was *completely impossible*.

After two or three years of Thatcher government, things were even worse than they appear in these figures. It wasn't just that unemployment rose and output fell. No statistics can truly represent the extraordinary devastation wrought on British industry. Apologists have tried hard to maintain that it was mainly or entirely weak firms that were weeded out. But that is not the case. There was a uniquely lethal combination of collapsed demand, very high interest rates, and a very high exchange rate. Some weak firms undoubtedly were destroyed. But so were a large number of extremely efficient firms. The most highly capitalized ones could afford neither to continue production nor to cease production and were driven into bankruptcy.

The early Thatcher years were accompanied by the most irritating rhetoric. On the one hand, there was the endless repetition of the phrase "There is no alternative," which soon acquired the acronym "TINA." On the other hand, there was the maddening repetition by Mrs. Thatcher herself to the effect that any attempt to cut unemployment would only generate a reduction in the short term and lead to "more later." The only thing is, we got more and more and more the later it got.

To me the explanations for inflation in the Thatcher period were quite simple. Inflation rose immediately after the government came to power because government immediately made a highly regressive switch from direct to indirect taxation. (Did they really think that raising indirect taxes would not raise prices because the money supply *alone* caused price changes?) And the fall in inflation was caused by the high unemployment.

As far as the falls in output and employment are concerned, surely this was the result (as I predicted with great emphasis at the time) of a very tight monetary policy—that is the huge rise in interest rates in the vain attempt to control the money supply—combined with a very tight fiscal policy. The disinflationary effects of tight monetary and fiscal policy were compounded by the fact that as a result of them (together with the adventitious rise in exports of North Sea Oil), the exchange rate soared about 30 percent, and this had the effect of reducing exports and export profits.

We now come to a matter that remains controversial.

In the spring of 1981, when output was collapsing and unemployment exploding, there was a tough, deflationary budget. This was still in a period when the sole instrument of macroeconomic policy was taken by the government to be the control of the money supply, with fiscal policy supposedly *wholly* subordinate to this end. It was absolutely clear to me that for as long as they stuck to their policy there would never, at any stage, be a real recovery in output, certainly not enough to generate a fall in unemployment.

The 1981 budget was the occasion for the drafting by two of my colleagues, Frank Hahn and Robert Neild, of a manifesto that was signed by 364 economists and that stated that continuation of the existing policies would deepen the depression, that deflation of demand would never produce a recovery in employment, and that there were alternatives. Let us see what happened next (Figure 2.11).

As can be seen, from early 1983 output rose strongly. That rise in output was the occasion for much Thatcherite triumphalism. The general view was, *and remains*, that the British economy was undergoing an economic miracle, and that the 364 economists had made utter fools of themselves.

Before coming to the analysis, note that from the beginning to the end of the Thatcher period, although output did rise, its average rate of growth was extremely small—slower, as a matter of fact, than in any pre-Thatcher period of comparable length. Conservative politicians always try to measure the performance of the economy from the trough—saying that starting from 1981 you have the fastest postwar growth rate. Looking at things that way, they could have had a faster growth rate still if output had fallen twice as much in the first two years.

The analogue chart for unemployment (Figure 2.12) displays some of the same properties of the output chart, with a substantial fall in unemployment beginning in mid-1986. Note that unemployment at the end is still much higher than it was at the beginning. It should also be noted that the figures had been fiddled in some important ways—for instance, by changing the basis of calculating unemployment from

Figure 2.11 **Manufacturing Output During Forty-Three Years**

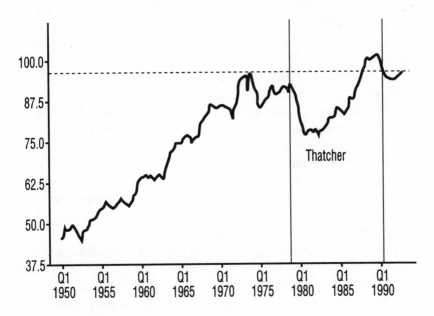

Figure 2.12 **Unemployment** (1950–90)

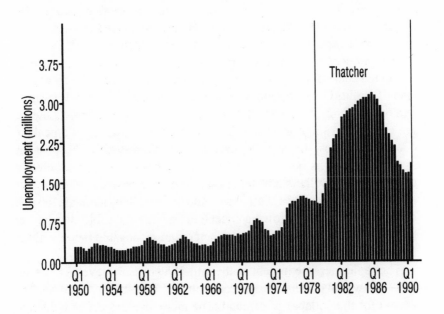

counting the number registering for jobs to the number who successfully claim unemployment benefits, and then making it much harder to
claim successfully.

The key question is, Why did the rise in output take place? Was it
the result of Mrs. Thatcher's policies winning through in the end?
Were we seeing the fruits of increased incentives and freeing the vital
energies of the British people, and so on? Did the 364 economists
really make fools of themselves? In fact, the 364 had not argued that
there would never be a recovery under *any* circumstances. They said
that *existing policies* would never generate a recovery. In fact, existing
policies were not maintained.

The Conservatives had only one macroeconomic policy—controlling the growth of the money supply. But that is what they conspicu-
ously failed to do (see Figure 2.13). Instead of coming down
progressively into the 6–7 percent range as "existing policies" had
decreed, the money supply grew ever faster into the 16–20 percent
range. This happened because the financial system was being totally
deregulated. In particular, all forms of control over consumer credit
and mortgage borrowing were removed. The counterpart of the growth
of the money supply was a sensational growth in the flow of net
lending to the household sector (see Figure 2.14). The flow of net
lending rose to nearly 20 percent of personal disposable income, far
larger than had occurred in the Heath-Barber boom of 1972–73. As if
that weren't enough, direct taxation was significantly relaxed.

In other words, we had the biggest "go" of all time. A good old-
fashioned consumer boom driven by combining tax cuts with an explosion of credit! Consumption rose 30 percent in the five years ending in
1989 (Figure 2.15). In the Heath-Barber boom the average rate of
growth of consumption over a four-year period had reached a peak of
4.4 percent. Now it hit 5.75 percent, more than double the postwar
average. This was not sustainable on the supply side, as was clearly
demonstrated by the sharp deterioration of the balance of payments
and the sharp upturn in inflation. And it wasn't sustainable on the
demand side either—growing indebtedness was a bubble that had to
burst, having risen by 1991 to 100 percent of disposable income, three
times the level in 1974 (Figure 2.16).

The rapid increase in debt in the mid-1980s finally leveled off after
1989. If we take the first difference in this increase, we can see the
reason for the collapse in demand. The mere leveling off of indebted-

Figure 2.13 **Growth Rate of Money Stock**

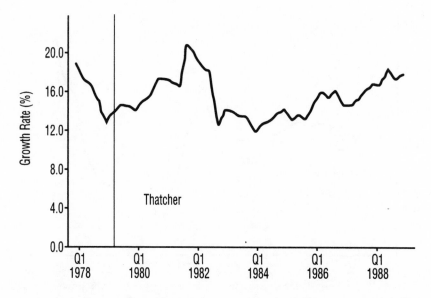

Figure 2.14 **Flow of Net Lending to Consumers as Percent of Disposable Income**

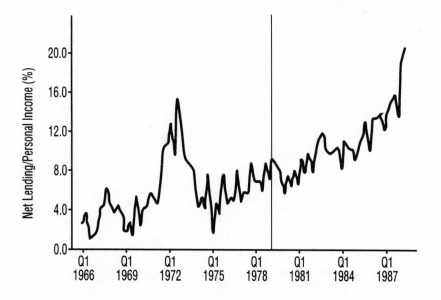

Figure 2.15 **Percent Change in Consumption in Successive Four-Year Periods[a]**

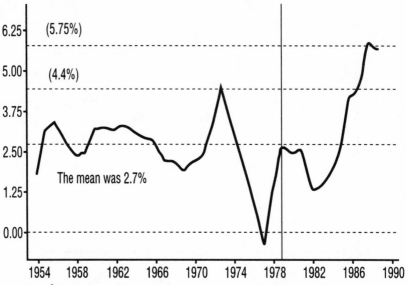

Note: [a]Each observation equals the percentage change over the previous four years.

Figure 2.16 **Household Debt as a Percent of Disposable Income**

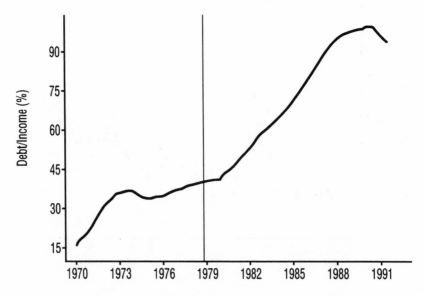

Figure 2.17 **Flow of Net Lending to Consumers as Percent of Disposable Income**

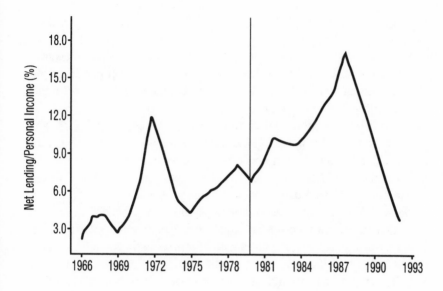

Figure 2.18 **Unemployment**

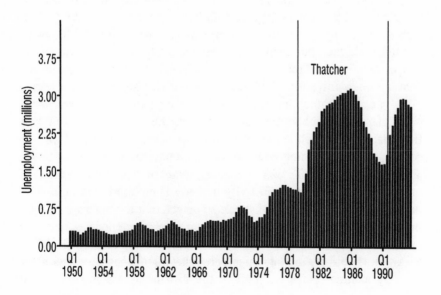

ness had as its logical counterpart a fall in the *flow* of credit from nearly 20 percent of personal disposable income to roughly *zero* (Figure 2.17). The result was a collapse in demand and output and a sharp increase in unemployment, which, in 1992, nearly reached 3 million once again.

We can now take stock, and look at the whole period since Mrs. Thatcher came to power in the context of the entire postwar period. We have already seen (Figure 2.11) what happened to the performance of manufacturing industry from 1950 to the end of 1992. As a result of Mrs. Thatcher's famous policy of "creating the conditions for stable growth," we had the slowest growth rate of the postwar era. The counterpart of that slow growth was a rise of unemployment to previously unimagined levels (see Figure 2.18)—punctuated only by the unsustainable consumption-driven boom of the late 1980s.

Slow growth and increasing unemployment were accompanied by a rundown of the productive strength of the economy. Investment in manufacturing, the vital component of the country's trade, reached postwar lows (Figure 2.19), and the declining competitiveness of Britain's manufacturing industry was manifest in persistent deterioration in the balance of payments, despite the surplus on trade in oil enjoyed in the early 1980s (Figures 2.20 and 2.21).

The true legacy of Mrs. Thatcher's policies is that the current position of the British economy, with unemployment around 10 percent of the labor force, must be regarded as the norm we now have to live with, *because the economy is severely supply constrained.* The proof of this is the fact that even in a recession the balance of payments is still in deficit to the tune of 2 percent of GDP. And there are reasonable grounds for supposing that capital investment of the relevant kind—i.e., that which enhances competitive supply—has been inadequate. The Lawson boom misdirected investment into distribution and financial services, while manufacturing investment fell. There was, of course, a significant improvement in manufacturing productivity in the Thatcher years, but *this was not accompanied by any increase in manufactured output.* The productivity increase is no good without an improvement in performance that can be detected at the macro level. An improvement in productivity without an improvement in output just means that there is more unemployment with nothing to show for it.

And it should always be remembered that all this has been accompanied by a huge regressive shift in the distribution of income. Most

Figure 2.19 **Manufacturing Investment as a Percent of GDP**

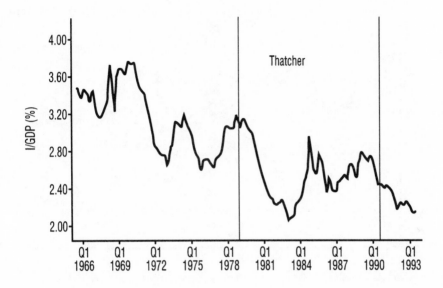

Figure 2.20 **The Current Balance of Payments** (as a Percent of GDP)

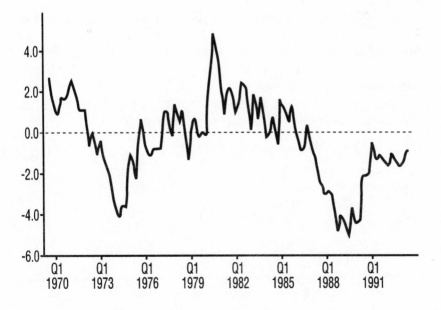

Figure 2.21 **The Current Balance of Payments, Oil and Non-Oil** (as a Percent of GDP)

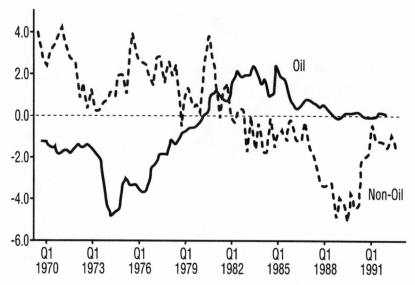

people have gone on getting better off. But a huge minority, one-fifth of all households, have seen their real incomes fall since 1979—many have suffered terribly.

This is the economic record of the British prime minister whom so many Americans profess to admire. If this American admiration for Mrs. Thatcher truly exists, I think Freud's diagnosis of why people do things and feel things is probably appropriate. Look what actually happened: the country was made weaker and poorer and far more divided. If this is admired, I can only conclude that it is a spectacle that affords some pleasure—the pleasure of Schadenfreude.

3

Convergence, Technological Competition, and Transmission of Long-run Unemployment

Alice H. Amsden

Faster Innovation, Slower Employment Growth

The decline of the United States as a hegemonic global economic power has been recognized as sufficiently consequential to redefine the structure of, say, world financial markets. But the decline of hegemony is also likely to affect domestic employment growth in industrialized countries through changes in the structure of technology generation.

Increasingly the world economy is characterized by "convergence" in productivity levels and (if somewhat belatedly) in technological capabilities (Baumol, Nelson, and Wolff, 1994). Many industrialized countries have begun to cluster around the world technological frontier, with none likely to enjoy anywhere near as big a lead over the others as the United States enjoyed in the three immediate postwar decades (Nelson, 1991). As geographical centers of best-practice innovation multiply, countries with more or less similar levels of wages and productivity may be expected to source more of their new products and processes from each other rather than from domestic suppliers. As competition among innovators reduces returns to innovation, strategic alliances among firms and among subsidiaries of the same multinational firm are likely to raise the number of collaborative innovation projects, as well as the rate of international technology diffusion. Therefore, we shall very likely see a rise in the number of world-class innovating countries, the overall rate of innovation, and the diffusion of innovations among countries.

Given these structural changes, the long-run growth rate of employment (and hence the unemployment rate) within this "convergence club" may be squeezed as never before. Any given attempt on the part of a single country to stimulate demand through macroeconomic policies will be more likely than otherwise to raise imports of innovative products from other countries rather than domestic output. More competition among countries may generate a larger number of innovations but, barring a remarkable technological breakthrough on a par with, say, the internal combustion engine or the transistor, will also generate a lower rate of return on investment for each innovation. In the case of product innovations, which historically have predominated over process innovations, shorter "product life cycles" and fewer monopoly rents are to be expected. Consumer welfare will rise as product innovations enhance product quality, but lower returns to innovating are also likely to exert a dampening effect on investments in new production capacity and, therefore, the growth of income and employment. Whereas monopoly rents from innovation in the United States during its Golden Age of technological hegemony fueled world expansion, the dispersion of innovation among many countries, with dwindling monopoly profits, is unlikely to be as expansionary.

As countries converge not just in technological capabilities and productivity levels but also in wages, there is also likely to be more intense competition to reduce costs. Hence, there is likely to be more effort invested in labor-saving process innovations. Furthermore, such process innovations may be expected to be disseminated more widely than before, as transactions in technology between firms and among subsidiaries of the same firm multiply. With strategic alliances among firms and the subsidiaries of the same firm raising the rate of technology diffusion, the process innovations of any one country are likely to circulate widely.

There will thus be a tendency for employment cutbacks and downsizing to accelerate unrelated to the usual channels through which foreign competition makes itself felt on domestic employment markets—imports and outward foreign investment (capital export). Increasingly, stimuli for downsizing will be transmitted *within* the multinational firms, or between independent firms from different countries organized in strategic alliances, as subsidiaries strive to reach best practice global technique. Any single country may find itself saving labor per unit of output without experiencing as much of a compensating increase in total income or number of employment hours as previously. Given more intersecting technology diffusion paths, tariffs to curb imports and controls to reduce capital export, if introduced, may be expected to have less chance of saving jobs.

The core issue just raised can be represented as follows. Let employment be N and output be Y such that:

$$N = aY$$

where a represents the average labor requirement per unit of output. Labor productivity is defined as the ratio of output to labor input. Given the newly emerging institutional structure of technological competition and collaboration among firms in different countries, the downward pressure on the coefficient a is likely to increase as the number of innovations rises, but with fewer offsetting tendencies for total output or employee hours to rise as well. Many countries will attempt to innovate, but due to competition, the return to total innovation will decline. The expansionary effect of this innovating pattern on the world economy, by comparison with the size of the effect when the United States was world hegemonic power, threatens to be less.

The Golden Age (1950–70)

American technological leadership is estimated to have emerged in the 1890s, when the United States overtook the United Kingdom in developing new products, processes, and indeed, whole industries (Chandler, 1990). According to Angus Maddison (1982):

> The emergence of the USA as the technical leader was due to the fact that it had huge natural resources of land and minerals, which by 1890 had been opened up by improvements in transport and the creation of a vast internal market whose population was much bigger than that of any of the advanced European countries, and was growing much faster. (p. 39)

After World War II, technological hegemony manifested itself in unambiguous leadership in radical innovation and in exports of high-technology products. For example, in the case of semiconductors, one of the critical innovations of the postwar electronics revolution, American companies were the first producers of eleven of thirteen major

Table 3.1

Variations in Growth Rates of Advanced Capitalist Countries Over Time, 1820–1989

(Annual Average Compound Growth Rates)

	1820–1870	1870–1913	1913–1950	1950–1973	1973–1979	1973–1989
GDP	2.1	2.5	1.9	4.9	2.5	2.6
Per capita income	1.1	1.4	1.2	3.8	2.0	2.1
Labor productivity[a]	—	1.6	1.8	4.5	2.7	2.3
Investment[b]	—	2.9	1.7	5.5	4.4	—
Exports	4.0	3.9	1.0	8.6	4.8	4.7

Source: Adapted from Maddison (1982, 1991). Arithmetic average for Australia, Austria, Belgium, Canada, Denmark, Finland, France, Germany, Italy, Japan, Netherlands, Norway, Sweden, Switzerland, United Kingdom, and United States.

[a] GDP per hour of work; 1973–87.

[b] Canada, France, Germany, Italy, Japan, United Kingdom, United States only.

product innovations and seven of nine major process innovations from 1950 through the late 1970s (Soete and Dosi, 1983).

American technological hegemony culminated in a Golden Age of capital accumulation lasting from roughly 1950 to 1973, the year of the first energy crisis. As Table 3.1 indicates, growth of gross domestic product (GDP), per capita income, labor productivity, fixed investment, and exports all grew faster in sixteen advanced capitalist countries during this period than in any other period.

The felicitous effects of U.S. technological hegemony on world growth may be understood in terms of the "product cycle" trade theory advanced by Raymond Vernon (1966). According to this theory, the beneficent global effects of innovation and trade stem from a continuous flow of innovations from leading countries (or a single country), and the sequential relocation of production, as specific innovations mature and then become standardized products, to countries located farther from the world technological frontier. All countries benefit in this global product life-cycle pattern. Innovators benefit from being pioneers. The next tier of countries (envisioned in the 1960s as mostly European) benefits as innovations are handed down from the leader(s) and provide the basis for domestic production and export further downstream. Finally, the least advanced countries benefit as products become mass-producible with large amounts of labor and ordinary machinery.

Table 3.2

Declining U.S. Technological Hegemony: Some Indicators

	U.S.	Japan	W.Ger	U.K.	Fr	Other
U.S. patents,						
1978, %	62.4	10.50	8.80	4.1	3.20	11.0
1988, %	52.0	20.70	9.40	3.30	3.40	11.2
Citation ratios for U.S. patents,						
1975–88	1.05	1.35	0.72	0.91	0.75	—
World exports						
technology-intensive shares		0				
1965, %	27.5	7.20	16.90	12.00	7.30	29.1
1987, %	20.6	18.90	16.40	8.00	8.50	27.6
GDP per person employed						
(U.S.=100)						
1950	100.0	15.20	34.50	53.80	38.10	—
1975	100.0	53.20	68.50	62.50	71.60	—
1989	100.0	72.70	82.00	71.50	85.90	—

Source: Adapted from United States National Science Foundation, Surveys of Science Resources Series, *International Science and Technology Data Update: 1991*, Special Report, NSF 91–309.

In this hierarchical scheme every country has its place, and each country reaps a reward from its place. The second tier of countries benefits directly from the process of "convergence"—as it adopts the same technology as the most advanced countries, its productivity grows relatively faster than that of the most advanced countries because its industries start from a lower productivity level, so their jump in productivity is greater (assuming, as does Abramovitz [1986], that countries have the requisite "social capabilities" to converge).

The relative decline in American technological hegemony, principally at the hands of Japan, has come more slowly than the convergence in productivity levels, as suggested in Table 3.2. Productivity convergence has been happening since the end of World War II, as measured by GDP per person employed, whereas convergence in various science and technology indicators has been more drawn out. The same was true of the catch-up experience of the United States vis-à-vis Britain—first came convergence in market competition and then, with a considerable lag, the overtaking of Britain by the United States in scientific indicators, as measured by Nobel prizes in physics, chemistry, and physiology or medicine. The research and development parts of R&D thus tend to behave in a distinct manner in the catch-up process. All the same, by the 1980s there were indicators of decline in American technological hegemony.

The United States' share of U.S. patents granted declined from 62.4 percent in 1978 to 52.0 percent in 1988. Not all patents are of equal importance, of course, so to assign a weight to different patents, a "citation index" was developed by Computer Horizons, Inc., for the American National Science Foundation. Cited patents show the previous achievements in related fields of invention that were taken into account in judging the novelty and significance of the patent application under review. According to Table 3.2, between 1975 and 1988, Japan's citation ratio index, 1.35, exceeded that of the United States, at 1.05. What is more, the U.S. index was fairly close to that of the UK and the Netherlands (not shown in the table), both at 0.91. Finally, Table 3.2 indicates world export percentage shares of technology-intensive products. The share of the United States fell from 27.5 percent in 1965 to 20.6 percent by 1987.

Many reasons were advanced for both the post-1973 productivity slowdown and the relative decline of the United States' economy. American industry's competitive erosion at the hands of Japan was attributed to Japan's industrial policies (see Johnson, 1982; Itoh et al., 1991), its superior production system (Schonberger, 1982), and its better labor relations (Dore, 1973). According to another set of hypotheses, America's relative decline was attributed less to Japan's superiority than to a natural erosion of the United States' competitive assets—raw materials no longer were a decisive competitive advantage, and the large American market was increasingly part of a still bigger global market that other countries could enjoy. Yet another interpretation was macroeconomic in emphasis. According to Maddison (1982):

> Since the Second World War the European countries and Japan have greatly reduced the productivity gap between themselves and the USA. Since 1973, US productivity growth has decelerated rather sharply. There has been some slowdown in other countries, too, but less dramatically than in the USA.
>
> The most fundamental reason for the erosion of US productivity leadership is that in the postwar period the European countries and Japan have run their economies at a much higher pressure of demand

than ever before; unemployment has been at very low levels; and this induced very high rates of investment. The US economy has not been run at such high steam. (pp. 41, 42)

Maddison thus suggests that owing to active demand management policies in Europe, productivity rose in tandem with high investment rates.

From the picture we painted earlier, still another explanation emerges for the slowdown. American technological hegemony supported a Golden Age of global growth. In parallel fashion, the decline of the United States as the single most important innovating power may be expected to contribute to slower growth worldwide. The reasons are explored below.

Technological Convergence and Competition

The effects of convergence on the configuration of world technological change and hence long-run employment growth are many, and two will now be singled out for consideration.

Convergence implies greater competition among equal economies, and greater competition may be expected to raise the rate of technological innovation. More competition among equals—with roughly the same wage rates, productivity levels, and technological capabilities—raises the number of countries investing in world-class, state-of-the-art innovation. Countries wishing to reach the world frontier have to invest in their own technology. Even to be included in strategic alliances to share technology, they have to bring state-of-the-art technology to the bargaining table. Thus, the number of countries investing in world-class R&D rises and so accordingly does the rate of innovation. On the positive side, a greater number of total innovations (assuming the total rises as the number of innovating countries rises) may be expected to expand world growth and employment. On the negative side, under global conditions of convergence the new structure of innovation may be expected to weaken this expansionary effect.

Two contractionary effects of convergence on long-run employment growth that will be discussed stem from: (1) the greater likelihood, given a larger number of innovating countries, that any single country will source its innovative products and processes from suppliers outside its national borders; and (2) the increasingly relevant distinction between borrowing foreign technology in order to "catch up," when the world frontier still lies at a distance and wage rates differ among countries, and borrowing technology to "keep up," when all countries are roughly at the frontier but one country begins to inch behind another.

A Less Virtuous Circle?

What if $1/a$, the labor productivity coefficient of a country, rises as a consequence of a labor-saving innovation that is first introduced by a foreign competitor? Does it make any significant difference to a country's growth rate of employment if an innovation is introduced offensively, by a pioneering firm in the country itself, or defensively, as a response on the part of a country's firms to an innovation first exploited by a competitor in another country? Clearly it does make a difference, in terms of a country's growth rate of imports or exports, although in the Kaldorian "virtuous circle" of output and labor productivity growth, the source of the new technology underpinning higher productivity is not given much consideration (we assume that the country that succeeds in inventing or innovating is also the country that reaps the rewards from pioneering, or being the first to commercialize a new technology).

Kaldor argued that labor productivity growth in technologically advanced economies could best be understood as a consequence of rapid increases in demand, particularly demand for manufactures (see the "Symposium" in the *Journal of Post-Keynesian Economics*, 1983). As income and output rise, Kaldor showed, labor productivity tends to rise due to higher physical investments embodying new technology, economies of scale, and learning by doing. Nevertheless, if a new technology is generated in another country, and that country is also first to reduce the price or raise the quality of its product, then the country attempting to raise domestic demand will be more likely than otherwise to increase expenditures for the product in question in the form of imports rather than domestic output. Kaldor's virtuous circle is less virtuous under these conditions.

The significance for employment growth of a country's being a pioneer and introducing new technology offensively, or a borrower, and introducing it defensively, is also evident from the other loop of

Kaldor's cumulative causation, when higher productivity induces higher output growth.

In the case where new technology is embodied in investment goods, the country that introduces a new technology offensively may be expected to experience an increase in output (and hence employment) for two distinct reasons. One reason output will increase is that investment, a component of output, has to increase in order to commercialize the new innovation. But because the country is a pioneer, it may also be expected to enjoy increasing global market share for its product as world demand responds to its lower prices or higher quality.

By contrast, the borrower of new technology may be expected to enjoy increasing income only if domestic investment rises as part of a defensive strategy of firms to adopt their competitor's technology and gain parity with it in costs and quality. The extra output stimulus of higher global market share will not be felt; indeed, the borrowing country's market share may not even recover its previous level. Moreover, if new technology is not embodied in new physical capital, but instead takes a disembodied form, say, in the case of an improved quality control management system, then the borrowing country may simply experience a rise in labor productivity with no offsetting effect on total employment of increased output. If the technology is labor saving, unit labor requirements may merely fall without necessarily any increase in total hours of work.

In terms of policy, conditions of convergence make it harder for an individual country to raise domestic demand alone, in isolation from competitors. When a single country tries to stimulate demand in the presence of a large number of countries innovating at the world frontier, it is more likely to import the innovations embodied in the products of another country than to acquire products produced domestically. International convergence in technological capabilities strengthens the need for coordinated international macroeconomic management.

Catching Up Versus Keeping Up

It is necessary to point out why being a technology borrower may be very growth-enhancing for a country under certain conditions (the second tier in Vernon's product cycle theory) but not under others.

Alexander Gerschenkron (1962) was one of the first economic historians to point out the virtues of being a latecomer and having the advantage of borrowing technology whose development costs were already borne by another country. The dynamic of convergence in productivity levels starting in the late nineteenth century among Britain, the United States, and continental Europe was driven by technology borrowing. The further behind (in terms of productivity level) a country, the faster its productivity growth rate when introducing the same technology as more advanced countries (Abramovitz [1994], examines some historical evidence). The industrialization experience of East Asia has been a pure case of learning, or borrowing already commercialized technology from industrialized economies (Amsden, 1991).

The difference between these cases and the one discussed above lies in relative wage levels. If a backward country (one not at the world technological frontier) can borrow foreign technology and equalize productivity with its overseas competitors, yet still enjoy a labor-cost advantage due to lower wages, its growth in output and employment will be enhanced by a rising global market share. This process, which may be called catching up, will stimulate investment in further capacity and lead to increases in employment. This was the case in Europe after World War II and remains the case throughout most of East Asia. By contrast, economic growth will not be enhanced as much, if at all, if a country borrows technology and equalizes not just productivity but also labor costs and profitability with an overseas competitor. In this process of keeping up, technology diffusion is not as expansionary because the borrower is acting defensively rather than developmentally and gains no market share. Thus, the contribution of foreign technology diffusion to economic growth depends on distance from the world technological frontier (Fagerberg, 1988). If a country is too close (or too far!) from the frontier, economic growth as a consequence of infusion (imitation) may be minimal, as in keeping up under conditions of convergence rather than catching up under conditions of divergence.

In conclusion, convergence may be expected to have a dampening effect on economic growth and, hence, long-run employment expansion, in both the country losing relative market share due to a decline in hegemony and the countries arriving at the world frontier. Table 3.3 compares the hypothetical situation under conditions of divergence, when a hegemonic power is responsible for all innovation (five in total) and four countries are attempting to catch up, and convergence,

Table 3.3

The Ratio of Innovations Pioneered to Innovations Infused: An Example Comparing Convergence and Divergence

Country	Innovation to Infusion Ratio	
	Divergence Catching Up	Convergence Keeping Up
1	5:0	5:20
2	0:5	5:20
3	0:5	5:20
4	0:5	5:20
5	0:5	5:20

when all five countries each pioneer five new innovations, but each infuses a total of twenty internationally.

In the case of Country 1, macroeconomic independence and economic growth may be expected to be less under "convergence" than under "divergence" because its ratio of "technologies pioneered" to "technologies infused" falls, from 5:0 to 5:20. In the case of Countries 2–5 as well, both macroeconomic independence and economic growth may be expected to decrease as they cease to enjoy the boost to productivity and market share that they once derived from borrowing state-of-the-art technology but retaining relatively low wage advantage. The gains from catching up fall to the next tier of countries—the East Asian late industrializers in the 1980s (Hikino and Amsden, 1994).

Technology Diffusion and Competition

Greater competition among firms from different countries, owing to convergence in levels of technological capabilities, holds different implications for consumers and producers. On the one hand, when competition rises, consumers tend to benefit from lower-priced or higher-quality products. On the other hand, producers tend to suffer from reduced profit margins, which, if they feed into lower investment rates, may hurt consumers indirectly, in their capacity as employees or corporate equity shareholders.

By the 1980s downward pressure on profitability from innovating may be inferred from shorter product life cycles. A product life cycle is defined as the span of time from the invention of a product through its introduction, growth of market, and maturation, and finally to its replacement by a new product. Product cycles were estimated to be growing shorter as greater global competition led to the faster substitution of existing products by newer and better (or at least different) ones (Abernathy and Hayes, 1980).

Simultaneously, the costs of doing research and development rose in the 1980s relative to the average price level. This inflation may have been inherent in the nature of R&D, which involved making one-of-a-kind prototypes and generally using processes that were intensive in highly skilled labor. By contrast, the average price level benefited from an increasing standardization of production, of both goods and services, which, as a result of innovation, tended to keep prices down. For example, the introduction of quartz technology transformed the making of watches into a scale-intensive, mass-production industry that lowered the production costs of "precision" time pieces. But innovation was not yet capable of standardizing the innovation process itself, and so costs of innovating tended to rise faster than the national inflation rate. In the extreme case of weapons, for example, the original F-18 fighter aircraft cost roughly $1 billion to develop during the late 1970s, while the B-2 stealth bomber, first flown in 1989, absorbed $22 billion of R&D funds (Scherer and Ross, 1990, p. 619).

The rising costs of and declining returns to innovating precipitated what has come to be called globalization or internationalization of R&D. According to two Harvard Business School professors:

> The increasing cost of R&D, coupled with shortening life cycles for new technologies and the products they spawn, has driven companies to seek global volume in order to amortize the heavy investment as quickly as possible. The high cost of product and process development has also encouraged companies to transfer new technologies voluntarily.
>
> Licensing has become an important source of funding, cross-licensing provides a means to fill technology gaps, and joint development programs and strategic alliances are emerging as a strategy for building global competitive advantage rapidly. (Bartlett and Ghoshal, 1989, p. 12)

In fact, some of what has been called globalism is merely "globaloney"—the extent to which the national economy has been superseded by the international economy is subject to hyperbole. Moreover, strategic alliances among innovators may reduce innovating costs, which may have the effect of offsetting declining returns to innovation and, hence, the need to internationalize. Nevertheless, it is unmistakable that collaborative R&D efforts and new attempts to manage multinational firms in a truly multinational manner have increased the rate of technology diffusion across borders. As Bartlett and Ghoshal observe: "Even the most advanced technologies have diffused rapidly around the globe" (1989, p. 12).

Technology flows—measured as (1) total world receipts of royalties and fees (say, for foreign licenses), (2) developed countries exports of capital goods, and (3) technical assistance to developing countries—rose from roughly $27 billion in 1962, to $92.2 billion in 1972, to $356 billion in 1982. This is a thirteenfold increase compared with only a threefold increase in the unit value index of all manufactures exported by developed countries over the same time period. Royalties and fees alone, although much smaller in total value than developed countries capital goods exports, tripled in value in the single decade between 1972 and 1982 (UNCTAD, 1987, p. 88).

As convergence increases the level of competition among countries, as technologies diffuse more readily and rapidly internationally, and as greater competition generates more investment in labor-saving process technologies—increasingly designed to save highly skilled managerial labor—the growth rate of employment, particularly white-collar employment, may be expected to decline. White-collar unemployment (defined to include professional specialty, technical, sales, administrative, and managerial employees) became a serious problem in many European countries in the 1980s and was recognized finally as problematic in the United States in the early 1990s. From the onset of recession in the first quarter of 1990 until the end of 1991, white-collar employment, which had continued to grow in the United States during previous recessions, was stagnant. During the same period, white-collar workers were added to the unemployment total at about the same rate as were blue-collar workers, an unprecedented development (Nasdone et al., 1992, p. 12).

The diffusion of technology through channels that are increasingly multinational further reduces the ability of individual national governments to influence domestic unemployment rates. More and more, the impact of foreign competition on domestic employment tends to be felt outside the policy sphere as traditionally defined, to include standard measures such as tariffs and capital controls designed to curb imports and check runaway plants. The impact of foreign competition on domestic employment is becoming a matter internal to the multinational firm or the multinational strategic corporate alliance. New multinational policies to stimulate employment growth will consequently be necessary. Attention is now turned to the mechanisms operating to increase international technology diffusion.

The Rate of Diffusion: The Multinational Firm

A large share of total world trade, including trade in capital goods—a major carrier of new technology—is accounted for by shipments between subsidiaries (including headquarters) of multinational firms. For instance, in the case of American multinational firms, in 1991 it was estimated that 62 percent of total U.S. merchandise exports and 44 percent of total U.S. merchandise imports were associated with American multinationals (Mataloni, 1993). In parallel fashion, U.S.-based affiliates of foreign companies also accounted for a large share of total U.S. merchandise trade. In 1991 nonbank U.S.-based affiliates accounted for 23 percent of U.S. merchandise exports and for 37 percent of merchandise imports, but only 5 percent of employment and 6 percent of gross domestic product (Zeile, 1993).

Foreign investment among the advanced capitalist economies has grown substantially ever since the end of World War II. But a third phase of internationalization emerged in the 1980s (Sharp, 1993). It was characterized by:

(1) a very fast growth rate of foreign direct (equity) investment from Japan;

(2) the end of a one-way flow of capital from the United States to the rest of the world and the growth of the United States as a major recipient of foreign investment from Japan and Europe (an investment "triad" emerged, as shown in Figure 3.1, with large flows of foreign investment from and to the United States, Europe, and Japan);

(3) growth of substantial foreign investment flows within each part of the triad, especially in the form of mergers and acquisitions after 1985 among European firms in different European countries.

What tends to be exaggerated about the multinational firm is the globalization of its R&D. This is evident from the European data of Patel and Pavitt (1991), who examine patents registered in the United States by foreign subsidiaries (as a share of a European country's total U.S. patenting) and patents registered in the United States by domestic

Figure 3.1 **Intra-Triad Foreign Direct Investment, 1988 and 1989**

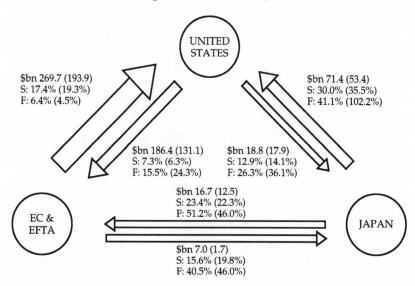

Source: UNCTC, *World Investment Reports* 1991 and 1992, United Nations.

Note: U.S. dollar figures are fore 1989 (1988) outward stock. Percentages show average annual growth rates, for stocks (S) and flows (F). Stock growth rates are for the period 1980 to 1989 (to 1988); flow growth rates are for the period 1985 to 1989 (to 1988). The data for United States outward and inward stocks in and from the EC and Japan include reinvested earnings.

firms (as a share of a European country's total U.S. patenting). With a few exceptions, most U.S. patenting in European countries was accounted for by domestically based and domestically owned firms. R&D continues to be done at home, a fortiori in the case of Japanese and American companies. In 1991 U.S. parents spent about $21 on R&D per $1,000 in sales compared with only about $7 for majority-owned foreign affiliates (Mataloni, 1993, p. 46).

Nevertheless, this pattern is changing. The R&D-intensity of majority-owned foreign affiliates of U.S. multinationals grew at 5 percent between 1982 and 1991, compared with only 3 percent for U.S. parents. This "partly reflects the formation of joint research ventures between majority-owned foreign affiliates and unaffiliated foreigners to help defray the cost of developing new technologies" (Mataloni, 1993, p. 46).

Thus, the rise of investment by foreign multinationals in the United States, the growth of intra-European foreign investment, and the faster growth rate of R&D accounted for by foreign affiliates all promise to increase the degree to which new technology is pumped across national borders by multinational companies, from subsidiary to subsidiary (including headquarters).

Of course, the mere existence of a multinational firm does not necessarily mean that technology will be diffused to all subsidiaries. Voluntarily or involuntarily, many multinational companies have a long history of allowing subsidiaries to operate with a high degree of autonomy. Coordinating international manufacturing and technology has been found to be a nontrivial challenge to management (Flaherty, 1986).

Nevertheless, there are an increasing number of examples of major companies that have begun to manage their international operations in a more coordinated fashion in order to survive new competitive challenges—a case in point being the Xerox Corporation, which confronted intense competition in the 1980s from the Japanese companies Canon and Ricoh. In response, Xerox began integrating much more tightly product design, best-practice manufacturing technique, and development of technological capabilities generally on a global basis (UNPTC, 1993, p. 124). Information technology itself has abetted such globalization. With such globalization, subsidiaries within a multinational organization are pressured to adopt the best-practice manufacturing technique, as each subsidiary maximizes its profits in order to compete for resources from headquarters. Such competition within the multinational organization occurs despite whatever monopoly power exists at the national level in traditional product markets.

Strategic Alliances and Diffusion

Another new aspect of internationalization in the 1980s related to the growth of strategic alliances among nationally independent firms. According to Sharp:

> In addition to foreign investment, other new forms of industrial linkage have become common—joint ventures, subcontracting, licensing, cooperative research agreements, second sourcing agreements. The result has been that many firms are now involved in complex international networks covering all the main areas of operation—research, production and marketing. (1993, p. 205)

According to Michael Porter and Mark Fuller:

> Coalition formation seems particularly related to the process of industry and firm globalization. When AT&T began to look outside its traditional U.S. market, for example, alliances with Olivetti and Philips were among its first moves. In the automobile industry, coalitions are widespread and include links between General Motors and Toyota and Isuzu, Ford and Toyo Kogyo [Mazda], Chrysler and Mitsubishi, and American Motors and Renault. In commercial airframes and engines, coalitions involve virtually every significant industry participant. (1986, p. 316)

In a study of 1,144 coalitions recorded by the *Wall Street Journal* between 1970 and 1982, Ghemawat, Porter, and Rawlinson found that "technology development was the governing motivation in 20 percent of the cases" (1986, p. 358).

If nothing else, strategic alliances among firms promise to hasten the diffusion of technology across national borders, hampering the ability of national governments to influence employment growth through demand management policies. To the extent that labor-saving process technologies are increasingly adopted by countries in reaction to adoption patterns in close competitor countries, the ability of national governments to control the growth rate of employment will become even harder.

Conclusion

Schumpeter "was right in asserting that perfect competition has no title to being established as the model of dynamic efficiency" (Scherer and Ross, 1990, p. 660). While strong monopolies and cartels do not have claim to that title either, we have argued that the process of convergence in technological capabilities among advanced capitalist countries since World War II promises to intensify competition among countries in the research and especially the development of new products and processes. This intensification of competition implies a larger number of countries engaged in R&D at the world technological frontier, a rising rate of innovation, and a rising rate of technology diffusion, all of which are positive. Yet it further implies a lower rate of return to innovation. Moreover, if one country tries to raise its domestic demand alone, it is more likely under conditions of convergence than divergence to increase demand for the products embodying innovations of other countries; imports rather than domestic output is likely to rise. Given increasingly multinational channels of labor-saving technology transfer, labor requirements per unit of output also promise to fall without any offsetting rise in the total number of labor hours employed.

The structural changes in technology generation implied by international convergence in productivity and innovative capabilities argue strongly in favor of greater coordination of expansionary macroeconomic policies among countries. There are sound purely macroeconomic reasons for favoring increased coordination. Technological reasons further strengthen the policy coordination case.

High unemployment rates among white-collar workers in Europe were all too familiar in the 1980s. Unemployment rates among white-collar workers as great as those among blue-collar workers first made their appearance in the United States in the recession beginning in 1990. As competition among countries at the world technological frontier intensifies further, greater attempts by corporations to downsize will increasingly affect managerial and administrative workers, and lower the employment level at which many corporations still believe there is fat to trim.

Macroeconomic policies alone will be inadequate to address the problems of rising white-collar unemployment. After all, when expansionary macroeconomic policies are adopted and corporate decisions are undertaken to invest in new production facilities, almost invariably large numbers of new production workers are required to construct and operate such facilities. But the amount of additional administrative labor required for such facilities may be negligible as corporations stretch the functions of existing white-collar staff, or introduce labor-saving information technology (Nell, this volume). Therefore, coordinating expansionary policies among countries to increase white-collar employment may require new solutions, such as large-scale international technology development projects, that are expanded or contracted in tune with the business cycle. It is noteworthy that the Uruguay Round of GATT negotiations outlawed subsidies to business by member countries in all areas except R&D. Therefore, one of the few areas still available for governments to introduce expansionary measures relates to R&D projects.

As convergence increasingly characterizes innovative capabilities among nations, innovative solutions to global employment problems will be required.

4

Free Trade, Unemployment, and Economic Policy

Anwar M. Shaikh

It is now widely recognized that a country's ability to compete effectively in the world market can be vital to its long-run prospects. Of course, in the short and medium run a country can protect itself from international competition through a variety of devices. Outright protection in the form of tariffs, quotas, and even subsidies can help insulate individual industries or regions. Manipulation of the exchange rate can enhance the competitiveness of national industries vis-à-vis the corresponding world sectors. And manipulation of the interest rate can induce foreign capital inflows and thus help cover any existing trade deficits. But in the long run, it seems, the issue of international competitiveness must be faced squarely.

Crucial questions are: how does opening up a country to international competition through free trade affect its levels of production and employment? Does free trade equalize competitive advantages, or does it worsen existing inequalities? Is laissez-faire the best way to participate in international trade, or is some degree of state support and management preferable?

The questions are age-old ones, and they involve both theoretical and policy considerations. To answer them adequately, we must address the actual workings of the capitalist world market. This means examining not only the *immediate* effects of international trade, but also the *longer-term* consequences, the ones that assert themselves through a slow and steady alteration of the initial effects, or by giving rise to unexpected or even unacceptable side effects. Successful policy therefore requires a structural analysis of international competition and the world market. In this regard, the analysis of the exchange rate is of critical importance, because it is the exchange rate that translates local costs and prices into the international arena (Chrystal and Sedgwick, 1989).

In what follows, we will examine the conventional views of the effects of free trade and international competition. We will then criticize these theories and present an alternate framework based on a structural approach to international competition.

Conventional Analyses of International Competition

Virtually all traditions of economics analyze competition within a single nation in roughly the same manner: as a process in which the strong firms win out against the weak ones. More specifically, within a given industry firms with lower unit costs are assumed to be able to beat out ones with higher costs. At the most abstract level of analysis, in which firms in the same industry are assumed to face the same wage and input costs, lower unit costs arise from greater efficiency in production. Efficiency can be broken down into efficiency in use of raw and auxiliary materials, efficiency in use of plant and equipment, and efficiency in use of labor. The overall effect can be summed up as "more advanced technology." At a more concrete level, where we consider firms located in different regions of the same country, or with differential access to segmented labor pools, the differential wage rates can also play an important role in influencing labor costs (Shaikh, 1991).

As long as the frame of reference is a single nation, then economic theories generally assume that competition is driven by the law of *absolute costs*, that is to say, firms with lower unit costs of production enjoy an absolute competitive advantage. Note that this particular outcome does not require full mobility of labor or even of investment capital. It requires only that customers will flock in greater numbers to firms with lower selling prices, and that investment funds will be more readily available to firms with higher profitability.

From this perspective, within any one country, high-cost regions would suffer from a competitive disadvantage. If unprotected, firms in such regions would tend to have declining shares in the national market. Their higher costs would make it difficult for them to sell outside the region and would leave their markets vulnerable to products produced in lower-cost regions. In other words, under unrestricted trade, high-cost regions would tend to have declining exports and rising imports relative to lower-cost regions. This in turn implies that if existing trade barriers were reduced among regions, the high-cost regions would tend to suffer job loss and a decline in real wages (due to both unemployment and to pressure from lower-wage regions).

The preceding implications are inherent in the very notion of competition and are common to virtually all schools of economic theory. But there are certain crucial respects in which conventional theory diverges from other approaches from this point onward.

To begin with, conventional economic theory asserts that full employment obtains within each country. Thus, increased interregional competition merely redistributes employment from less competitive to more competitive regions. Given full employment, the possibility of overall job losses is automatically excluded. Needless to say, theories that do not assume automatic full employment yield a very different perspective.

The orthodox treatment of competition between countries (i.e., of international trade) is even more curious. Here, it is argued that the existence of separate national currencies changes the very nature of competition itself: whereas orthodox economics concludes that national competition is ruled by absolute costs, it has always insisted that international trade is ruled by *comparative costs*.

The argument is well known and need only be sketched here. Consider the case of two countries, one of which has higher costs of production (due to lower productivity and/or higher wages) at some initial exchange rate. Now imagine what would happen if international trade is initiated between the two countries. In the case of fixed exchange rates, the country with an initial absolute disadvantage (higher unit costs) in international trade will suffer a balance of trade deficit, which will in turn lead to a money outflow to pay for this deficit. Orthodox economics assumes that this money outflow will lower the national price level in the deficit country. As prices fall, the industries with the least initial disadvantage (i.e., the "comparative advantage") will be the first to get back into competition, and the process will continue until enough of the country's industries become competitive to ensure that overall trade is balanced.

In the case of flexible exchange rates, it is the exchange rate that supposedly does the adjusting. As before, the absolutely disadvantaged country initially suffers a balance of trade deficit. But now this leads to the depreciation of its currency, which in turn lowers the foreign currency equivalents of its product prices. The process is assumed to continue until, once again, enough of the country's industries are competitive to ensure that trade is balanced.

The two cases above can be summarized by noting that in either scenario it is the *real exchange rate* that is assumed to move in such a way as to balance automatically the trade of every country, thereby making *all nations equally "competitive" in international trade, regardless of how backward their technology or how high their wages* (Officer, 1976, pp. 10–13; Arndt and Richardson, 1987, pp. 12–13). Moreover, since full employment is always assumed to hold, there can be no question of net job loss for either country. (Strictly speaking, it is assumed that any decline in employment is purely voluntary, on the grounds that under changed circumstances some workers may prefer not to work and hence voluntarily withdraw from the labor market. Nonetheless, markets clear.)

If it is assumed that international competition requires producers of the same good to sell at roughly the same price in common currency, after allowing for transportation costs, taxes, and tariffs, then the conventional argument depicted above also implies some version of the theory of Purchasing Power Parity (PPP): i.e., that price levels will be roughly similar in all nations when expressed in common currency. Some authors emphasize the general price level (Schumpeter, 1954, p. 1106), while others emphasize the price level of tradable goods alone (Harrod, 1933, pp. 53–63; Marston, 1987; Kravis and Lipsey, 1987; Dornbusch, 1988). Some even argue that PPP theory implies that unit *costs* of production will be equalized across countries, so that the automatic mechanisms of free trade end up making all countries truly equal in competition (Officer, 1976, pp. 10–12).

In theoretical models, it is often assumed that the real exchange rate is precisely at the trade-balancing level. It is, of course, understood that any actual balancing process would take time. Thus, at the empirical level the basic expectation of orthodox international trade theory is that

> [even though] an economy's international competitiveness might rise and fall over medium-term periods . . . on average, over a decade or so, ebbs and flows of competitive "advantage" would appear random over time and across economies. (Arndt and Richardson, 1987, p. 12)

At a more concrete level of analysis, orthodox theory takes up the question of international capital flows and their effect on the exchange rate. In the absence of capital flows, the balance of trade is the same thing as the balance of payments, and since it is assumed that the real exchange rate moves to equalize the former, it also automatically equalizes the latter. Once capital flows are considered, the same reasoning leads to the conclusion that the real exchange rate moves to equilibrate the overall balance of payments. In the face of exogenous capital inflows, this implies that the real exchange rate would move to accommodate these inflows by giving rise to a deficit in the trade balance, so that the overall payments are balanced (Rueff, 1967, p. 125; Krueger, 1983, p. 106). But the important point here is that insofar as the capital inflows arise in response to real interest rate differentials between countries, they will serve to arbitrage these differences and hence tend to eliminate them—which in turn will eliminate the need for the capital flows themselves. Therefore, although exogenously induced capital flows might disturb the process in the short and medium runs, it is expected that over the long run "trade will be balanced so that the value of exports equals the value of imports" (Dernburg, 1989, p. 29). In other words, in the long run international trade will operate as if nations "barter" exports for imports of equal value (Dornbusch, 1988, p. 3).

In sum, conventional theory concludes that neither technological backwardness nor high costs are ultimately a disadvantage in international trade. Real exchange rates will always move in such a way as to make all trading partners equally competitive, so that no country will suffer persistent trade deficits or enjoy persistent trade surpluses.

The trouble with all of this is that it has never fitted the facts. In the postwar period, for instance, neither competitive advantages, nor trade balances, nor even overall payment balances have been the least bit random across time or across economies. On the contrary, international trade has been characterized by "persistent, marked competitive advantage for [countries such as] Japan and marked competitive disadvantage for countries [such as] the United States," coupled with "persistent, marked trade balance surpluses for Japan and deficits for the United States." As some orthodox economists themselves admit, such patterns have served to undermine confidence in the traditional arguments (Arndt and Richardson, 1987, p. 12).

For a while it was thought that the fixed-exchange-rate system of the Bretton Woods was the explanation for this marked discrepancy between conventional theory and the facts. It was therefore widely expected that the switch to flexible exchange rates after 1973 would finally confirm the basic hypotheses of orthodox trade theory. But the results have been quite the opposite. Not only have persistent international imbalances failed to disappear, they have actually intensified. Moreover, it has rapidly become apparent to the best practitioners of orthodox economics that their theories are not able to explain the observed movements in flexible exchange rates. Dornbusch, who is one of the most influential voices in the field, has this to say:

> After twenty or thirty years of exchange rate modelling . . . we are left with the uncomfortable recognition that our understanding of exchange rate movements is less than satisfactory. Most models have lost their ability to explain what has happened, when exchange rates moved a lot, as in the 1980's. (Dornbusch, 1988, pp. 1–2)

The persistent discrepancies between orthodox theory and the historical facts have created great difficulties for the theory of international trade. In an effort to deal with this, two different tendencies have emerged. By far the dominant one has been to insist that the basic results still hold, but only in the long run. The observed discrepancies between the data and "the 'fundamentals' suggested by theoretical models of the exchange rate" (Dornbusch, 1988, p. 9) are then addressed as short- or medium-run phenomena. The four competing explanations in this vein are the monetary approach, the new classical approach, the equilibrium approach, and what Dornbusch calls the macroeconomic approach (ibid., p. 10). As the preceding quote from Dornbusch makes clear, he concludes that these models do not work well.

The other main reaction to the empirical difficulties of orthodox theory has been to try to make comparative cost theory "more 'realistic' " (Dosi, Pavitt, and Soete, 1990, p. 18) by relocating it within imperfect or monopolistic competition in the context of technological differences, economies of scale, differentiated products, multinational corporations, and so on. However, certain core assumptions concerning the behavior of maximizing agents and the automatic clearing of all markets are retained, even though they "are difficult to accept on either theoretical or empirical grounds" (ibid., p. 24). Most important, the central assumption that international trade is regulated by comparative costs remains unchallenged.

The Impact of Theory on Policy:
The Case of NAFTA

Given the difficulties with orthodox trade theory, one would think that empirical studies and policy analyses would be undertaken within alternate frameworks. But the hold of the theory is so great that one finds just the opposite: most empirical studies take the basic propositions for granted.

The debate around NAFTA is a good case in point. It was widely reported that three hundred prominent economists, ranging from conservatives to liberals, publicly endorsed NAFTA. Most studies also concluded that the United States, Canada, and Mexico will all benefit in terms of employment, wages, and lowered prices (Faux and Lee, 1993, pp. 2–6). Indeed, in October 1993 the White House issued a statement to the effect that "19 of 20 comprehensive studies" had concluded that NAFTA would benefit the United States (JEC, 1993, pp. v, xv).

But closer examination of these studies reveals that they simply assume that labor always remains fully employed, at least in the United States (JEC, 1993b, p. 12; Stanford, 1993, pp. 98–100). *Thus job loss is ruled out by assumption.* This is, of course, a reflection of a basic tenet of conventional economic theory. However, one can question whether it is appropriate to build such an assumption into empirical studies that purport to guide economic policy in the present-day world.

Most studies also assume that no investment will be diverted from the United States to Mexico. This, too, derives from the basic theory, since as we have seen, orthodox theory assumes that in the long run there will be no net capital flows between countries. Once again, it is difficult to justify such an assumption on empirical grounds, given that "the fundamental economic purpose of NAFTA is to facilitate the shift in investment to Mexico" (Faux and Lee, 1993, p. 11). Within Mexico, the openly declared official position is that the agreement will lead to a massive inflow of foreign investment. Many in the business community look upon the low wages and high potential productivity of Mexican workers as a great incentive for investment, particularly when coupled with a promised codification of liberal foreign trade and investment policies, permission for foreigners to enter into previously protected areas such as agriculture and oil, enforcement of international standards on patent and copyright laws, and notoriously poor treatment of labor and of the environment (Faux and Lee, 1993, p. 12; Koechlin et al., 1993, pp. 60–61; Stanford, 1993, p. 101).

Models that embody such standard neoclassical assumptions do not perform well in predicting actual outcomes. In the previous instance of the 1989 U.S.-Canada Free Trade Agreement (FTA), standard models turned out to be seriously deficient. Their predictions ranged from that of no significant change in Canadian manufacturing employment to that of increases on the order of 16–21 percent. The actual result turned out to be a severe employment decline of 14 percent (Stanford, 1993, p. 101). It is useful to note that models that do not simply assume, a priori, that there is full employment in each country and capital immobility between countries, end up predicting substantially different and more negative outcomes (JECb, 1993, p. 34; Stanford, 1993, p. 104).

Allowing for the possibility of unemployment and capital flows is a step in the right direction. But I would argue that this is not sufficient so long as the underlying theoretical structure is premised on the notion that competition between nations, unlike that within a nation, is essentially an equalizing process. This characteristic duality in orthodox theory is rooted in the claim that competition within a nation is regulated by absolute costs, while that between nations is regulated by comparative costs. It is supported neither by historical evidence nor by policy experience. If this basic proposition is indeed unsound, then substituting oligopoly theory for that of competition, or even relaxing the assumptions of full employment and lack of international capital mobility, may not be sufficient. Particularly if we aim to ground economic policy in the actual forces at work, it may be better to start from a different foundation. This is the issue to which we turn next.

An Alternate Approach to the Theory of International Competition

The approach presented here is an extension of earlier arguments (Shaikh, 1980, 1991). It has its roots in the classical tradition and in some recent empirically grounded approaches in the post-Keynesian, structuralist, and historical traditions. For instance, Adam Smith believed that international trade would operate in essentially the same manner as national trade: i.e., that it would be regulated by the absolute cheapness of the products involved, as determined by "natural or acquired" advantages (Allen, 1967, pp. 53–56; Dosi, Pavitt, and Soete, 1990, pp. 29–30). This is basically the law of absolute costs. It is Ricardo who substituted the law of comparative costs, although he did retain the idea that there exist persistent technological differences between nations. In more recent times, the assumption of different technological conditions reappears within the work of Dornbusch, Fisher, Samuelson, Posner, Vernon, and many others (Dosi, Pavitt, and Soete, 1990, pp. 21–22, 25–26). Finally, it is a widespread assumption in the classical, marxian, and neoricardian literature that real wages are primarily determined by forces within a country, and that the full employment of labor is not an automatic outcome (Emmanuel, 1972, ch. 3).

To ground the argument developed here, we return to the theory of comparative costs. We begin with the familiar situation of fixed exchange rates, in which the country with less efficient technology and/or relatively higher wages suffers an absolute disadvantage in international trade. It therefore experiences a persistent deficit in the balance of trade, with a corresponding persistent outflow of money to pay for this trade deficit. According to conventional analysis, the outflow of money will lower the price level in the country, thereby making it more competitive in international trade, until the point is reached where it is sufficiently competitive to achieve balanced trade. All of this is supposed to be automatic. In the end, high domestic costs are no real handicap in international trade (Feldstein, 1993, p. 4).

Many authors reject the monetarist foundation, which is the crucial link in the preceding argument (Moore, 1988; Wray, 1990). For instance, Harrod argues that the primary effect of a money outflow is to make the economy less liquid, which in turn tends to raise interest rates above the international level. Insofar as investment is at all sensitive to the interest rate, output and employment may fall, rather than prices (Harrod, 1933, p. 53; Keynes, 1936, p. 348). In any case, the resulting discrepancy in international interest rates will tend to attract short-term capital into the country, thus *covering up* the structural trade imbalance with international borrowing. This is evidently a limited solution, since it merely transforms the structural trade problem into one of rising international indebtedness, with all its attendant difficulties and limits. Of course, if the government acts to prevent interest rates from rising, it must then support the currency by running down reserves (devaluation is addressed below), or directly intervene by restricting imports and stimulating exports, or seek long-term capital inflows and/or foreign assistance to finance the trade deficit. But as long as the root cause, the relatively high unit costs of national industry, are not altered, the problem will reappear when such devices are exhausted.

Standard theory also tells us that balanced trade can be restored by devaluing the currency (in the case of fixed exchange rates) or allowing it to depreciate (in the case of flexible exchange rates). But the well-known difficulties with this approach are equally severe. First of all, insofar as devaluation or depreciation is successful in lowering the foreign currency equivalent of export prices (i.e., in causing the terms of trade to fall), this lowers export revenues and hence worsens the balance of trade at any given level of exports and imports. To offset this effect, export levels must rise and/or import levels must fall by sufficient amounts so as to improve the overall trade balance. This is the famous Marshall-Lerner-Robinson-Metzler "elasticities problem" that has so bedeviled the neoclassical literature. At best, it leaves us with the conclusion that the effects of devaluation and depreciation are theoretically indeterminate. But no such indeterminacy exists in the empirical record, since as we have already noted, the flexibility of exchange rates in the latter half of the postwar period has not led in any way to balanced trade among nations (Dornbusch, 1988).

Considerations such as these suggest that a reexamination of the theory of comparative costs might prove fruitful. A formal model of an alternate approach appears in Shaikh (1991) and is tested against the empirical experience of five advanced industrial countries (United States, Canada, United Kingdom, Germany, Japan). Here, we only outline the basic steps in the argument.

First, it is an essential feature of our analysis that production conditions and real wages are assumed to differ across countries. Neoclassical theory tends to assume that production functions are similar across countries, and even derives a fundamental theorem that factor prices (i.e., wages and interest rates) will therefore be equalized, through international trade alone, across countries (Leontief, 1985, p. 377). Yet nothing could be further from the empirical facts. Production conditions and real wages have always varied considerably across countries throughout the history of capitalism.

Although this point was already an essential part of the classical tradition, it has recently been emphasized once again. Dollar, Wolff, and Baumol (1988) find that for any given industry, productivity varies substantially across countries, with an average variation of 100 percent (p. 31, Table 2.1). For any given international industry, such international productivity variations are largely explained by corresponding variations in real capital-labor ratios. Moreover, countries with higher productivity and/or capital-labor ratios in one industry tend to have higher measures in all industries (p. 33, Table 2.3), and countries with higher productivity in a given industry tend to also have higher wages in the same industry (p. 42). On this basis we assume that real wages and technology are determined locally in each nation. Of course, money wages can be sticky in the short run. But it is expected that in the long run the key determinants of the real wage are factors such as national productivity, output growth, level of unemployment, and balance of forces between workers and their employers. This also implies that the real wage is not necessarily a market-clearing variable, so that full employment of labor is not presumed—unlike conventional models, in which the real wage is assumed to move in such a way as to make trade balanced or to bring about the full employment of labor (Krueger, 1983, pp. 159–60; Dornbusch, 1988, p. 5).

Second, it is assumed that international competition *binds together* the prices of internationally traded commodities. We will call this the Law of Correlated Prices (LCP). Note that this does not require an immediate and complete international equalization of the prices of a common good, as is often assumed in the conventional notion of the Law of One Price (LOP). For one thing, the existence of transfer costs (transport, insurance, etc.) and of tariffs and taxes implies that there exists a band within which a country's producers are insulated from international competitive pressure, but outside of which competition begins to assert itself. This band of "commodity points" is similar in nature to that of "gold points" under the gold standard. Leontief (1985, pp. 379–80, Tables 1–2) estimates that transfer costs can be substantial, so that when one also adds in tariffs and taxes, it is certain that the band in question is quite wide. Inside this band, local factors will determine the location and movements of a commodity's price. Outside of it, international competition will become the dominant influence. It is therefore hardly surprising that the empirical evidence rejects the notion that international prices are precisely equal at all times (Levich, 1985, pp. 1002–6). But if one views the LCP as a longer run process subject to commodity point bands, the evidence is much more support-ive. Crouhy-Veyrac (1982), Crouhy and Mélitz (1982), Aizenman (1986), and Protopapadakis and Stoll (1986) all show that the presence of commodity points implies an essentially nonlinear process of adjust-ment, and that conventional tests will reject the LCP even when it is in fact true. Since conventional price data do not include estimates of the actual bands involved, Protopapadakis and Stoll (1986) test a nonlinear process of adjustment on the data and conclude that (viewed in this way), "The long run Law of One Price is a usable approximation of the behavior of commodity prices for macroeconomic purposes" (p. 350). In a similar vein, McCloskey and Zecher (1985) argue that the LCP should be understood as implying "a close correlation among [corre-sponding] price levels brought about by the ordinary workings of mar-kets" (p. 66). They find that even as early as 1880–1913, in the period of the gold standard, there is a high correlation between British and American prices and interest rates (pp. 64–73).

The hypothesis of roughly similar prices (in the above sense) does not tell us anything about the common level around which the prices gravitate. Thus, a third hypothesis is required, linking the price struc-ture to the international costs of production for any particular product. There are two parts here.

To begin with, we argue that international competition behaves in the same way as national competition, in that producers with lower unit costs will be able to cut prices and expand their market share at the expense of their less fortunate rivals. It is implicit here that we are speaking of prices adjusted for quality differences, because a higher quality product offered at the same price is equivalent to a cut in prices for a given quality. In speaking of producers with lower costs, it is important to note that if these costs are to be effective in driving prices, the supply from these producers must be capable of being expanded. Thus, it is producers with the lowest generally reproducible cost struc-tures who will be able to drive the market price of products. We will call them the *regulating producers* for a given international commod-ity. (In case of agricultural and natural resource production, the regu-lating producers will be the lowest cost producers on the best land still available, the latter being in general on the margin of cultivation.)

We further specify the link between market prices and the unit costs of the regulating producers by assuming that relative prices can be well approximated by the relative *total (i.e., direct and indirect) unit labor costs of the regulating producers*. The term total unit labor cost refers to the product of the money wage w and the total unit labor requirement λ, the latter being what is often called the vertically integrated labor coefficient (Milberg and Elmslie, 1992, p. 103). This result can be derived either from a classical framework, along the lines of Ricardo, Sraffa, and Pasinetti, or from a mark-up pricing framework as in Eichner (Shaikh, 1984; Milberg and Elmslie, 1992). It has strong empirical support (Ochoa, 1988; Bienenfeld, 1988).

In the international context, the two preceding assumptions translate into the proposition that countries with reproducibly lower total real unit costs (e.g., Japan and Korea) will have dynamic and growing export markets. More formally, we can derive several specific results concerning the determinants of real exchange rates, trade patterns, and the competitive position of various countries in the world order (Shaikh, 1991).

The Law of Correlated Prices implies that the prices of a given commodity are roughly equal across nations (in the sense specified earlier), when expressed in common currency. We can also say that for any given commodity the international currency price (p') is therefore roughly equal to the price ($p^{*\prime}$) set by the regulating producer, where the superscript * refers to the regulating producer and the apostrophe refers to money magnitudes expressed in a common international currency. Accordingly, the average price of country i's bundle of tradable goods will be roughly equal to the average regulating price of this same bundle, in common currency. It follows that the ratio of the average prices of tradables in countries i and j will roughly equal the ratio of average regulating prices of the corresponding bundles: (p_i'/p_j') ($p_i^{*\prime}/p_j^{*\prime}$). Finally, since relative regulating prices can be closely approximated by the relative total unit labor costs of the regulating producers, we can also write: ($p_i^{*\prime}/p_j^{*\prime}$) ($v_i^{*\prime}/v_j^{*\prime}$), where $v^{*\prime} = (w^{*\prime})\lambda^* =$ total unit labor cost and $w^{*\prime} =$ the money wage, in common international currency, and $\lambda^* =$ the total or vertically integrated labor coefficient, *of the regulating producers*. Putting all of this together allows us to link the relative prices of the tradable goods of any two countries i and j to the total unit labor costs of the *regulating* producers of the two corresponding bundles of tradables, all expressed in a common currency.

$$(p_i'/p_j') \cong (p_i^{*\prime}/p_j^{*\prime}) \cong (v_i^{*\prime}/v_j^{*\prime}) = (w_i^{*\prime}/w_j^{*\prime})(\lambda_i^*/\lambda_j^*) \qquad (1)$$

Notice that equation 1 tells us that the average price of any two bundles of tradable goods will be equal only when the bundles are the same (in which case $w_i^{*'} = w_j^{*'}$ and $\lambda_i^* = \lambda_j^*$).

We have already argued that real wages are primarily determined by forces within a given country. If we represent real wages by wr, and the price of tradable consumption goods by pc, then the relative money wages of the regulating producers of tradable bundles i and j, expressed in a common currency, can be written as $(w_i^{*'}/w_j^{*'}) = (wr_i^*/wr_j^*)(pc_i^{*'}/pc_j^{*'})$. But if the bundles of tradable *consumer* goods are similar across countries (the extension to nontradables is addressed in Shaikh, 1991), $pc_i^{*'} \cong pc_j^{*'}$, so that

$$(w_i^{*'}/w_j^{*'}) = (wr_i^*/wr_j^*)(pc_i^{*'}/pc_j^{*'}) \cong (wr_i^*/wr_j^*) \qquad (2)$$

Equation 2 says that the common currency relative money wages of the regulating producers of bundles i and j are essentially determined by the relative *real* wages of these collections of producers. This implies that common currency relative money wages and hence *relative unit labor costs are independent of the exchange rate*, in the long run. Of course, since money wages are sticky in the short run, exchange rate variations can affect the real wage and real unit labor costs through their effects on the prices of consumer goods. But in the long run these variables will be nationally determined (by the nations in which the regulating producers of a given bundle are located).

Since all of our propositions have been in terms of general bundles of tradable goods, we can express them equally well in terms of the exports and imports of any given country. Equations 1 and 2 then immediately yield the proposition that *the long-run terms of trade of a country are independent of its exchange rate*. Let px', pm' represent common currency export and import prices, respectively.

$$(px'/pm') \cong (wr_x^* \lambda_x^*)/(wr_m^* \lambda_m^*) \qquad (3)$$

The left-hand side of equation 3 is the terms of trade of a given country while the right-hand side represents the ratio of the regulating unit labor costs of its export and import bundles, respectively. But the latter is cast entirely in terms of real variables and is therefore independent of exchange rates.

An equivalent expression can be written for the ratio of common currency prices of the tradables of any two countries i and j, by directly combining equation 1 and 2. Since the common currency price ratio is merely the local currency price ratio (p_i/p_j) divided by the nominal exchange rate ratio $e_{ij} = (e_i/e_j)$, the nominal exchange rate e_i being defined here as units of local currency i per unit of international reference currency. This makes it analogous to the real exchange rate $er_{ij} = e_{ij}/(p_i/p_j)$. Thus, if country i is Japan, and the U.S. dollar is the reference currency, then e_i = yen/$. Note that a rise in the nominal or real exchange rate implies a *depreciation* of the currency, since more yen are required to purchase a dollar.

$$(p_i/p_j)/e_{ij} = (p_i'/p_j') = (w_{ri}^{*}\lambda_i^{*})/(w_{rj}^{*}\lambda_j^{*}) \tag{4a}$$

$$er_{ij} = \frac{e_{ij}}{(p_i/p_j)} \cong \frac{1}{(wr_i^{*}\lambda_i^{*})/(wr_j^{*}\lambda_j^{*})} \tag{4b}$$

$$e_{ij} = \frac{p_i/p_j}{(wr_i^{*}\lambda_i^{*})/(wr_j^{*}\lambda_j^{*})} \tag{4c}$$

Equations 4a to 4c are equivalent, but they tell us different things. Equation 4a says that the common currency prices of the tradables of two countries are determined by the real cost conditions of the regulating producers of these bundles, and are independent of the exchange rate, in the long run. Equation 4b shows that the real exchange rate varies inversely with the real costs of the regulating producers involved (which need not be the countries i and j themselves). It follows from this that the real exchange rate can have a trend in the long run, depending on the movements of the real regulating costs. As we have seen, this implies that (absolute) Purchasing Parity would not hold even in terms of tradable goods alone, except in the case where both countries have similar baskets of tradables (so that the right-hand side of equation 4b is simply one). Finally, equation 4c shows us that the nominal exchange rate between any two countries will depend on two sets of factors: their relative nominal price levels, as expressed in their local currency tradable price ratio p_i/p_j; and inversely on the real costs of the regulating producers of the tradable goods of the two countries, as expressed in their real vertically integrated unit-cost ratio $(wr_i^{*}\lambda_i^{*})/(wr_j^{*}\lambda_j^{*})$.

Equation 4c also leads to another important conclusion. If we take the rates of change of both sides, we find that the rate of change of the nominal exchange rate equals the difference between the relative inflation rates of the two countries and the relative rates of change of the real total unit costs of the regulating producers. Real unit costs change at a slow but steady pace, so that in the short run relative unit costs are limited in their variation. But the same is not true of relative inflation rates. Thus, one would expect that when a country has a high relative inflation rate, the changes in its nominal exchange rate would be dominated by its relative inflation rate. But when relative inflation rates are low, then the slower movement of relative real costs could dominate. In other words, the *relative* version of PPP theory would appear to work well when countries experience high inflation rates, but would not work well in the opposite case. This addresses an enduring puzzle in the empirical and theoretical literature (Barro, 1984, p. 524, Table 20.4; Frenkel, 1978).

The fact that the terms of trade of a country are independent of the exchange rate in the long run (see equation 3) implies that international trade will give rise to *structural* trade deficits or surpluses that reflect the competitive position of the country involved. The relative trade balance is the product of the terms of trade p_x'/p_m' *and the export-import ratio X/M*. But in the long run *X/M* itself depends on the terms of trade and on the country's relative growth rate (a higher relative growth rate increases the growth of import demand relative to that of exports and thus worsens the balance of trade). If the terms of trade are indeed independent of the exchange rate in the long run, then (barring structural changes) a country can improve its trade balance only by *lowering* its relative growth rate. But if deficit countries cut their rate of growth in order to lower their relative import demand, the surplus countries (from which the deficit countries get their imports) would also suffer a decline in growth. The competitive differences would not be eliminated, so the structural imbalances in trade would reappear— only now at a lower overall rate of growth.

Another way of looking at this result is to recognize that real exchange rates depend on real relative costs (see equation 4b), i.e., on the relative competitive position of a country. Since real unit costs will differ across nations, structural trade balances will be "normal" in free trade.

The relation between competition and market shares requires further elaboration. When a firm lowers its selling price, two things happen: it attracts to itself customers from other firms (demand switching), and it attracts to itself customers who are new to the market (demand expanding). Both can have a large impact on the sales of an individual firm or region, even if the effect on the remaining firms or regions, or on the market as a whole, is initially small. The orthodox theory of "perfect competition" does away with the demand switching effect by simply assuming that firms never try to undercut their competitors' prices—i.e., by assuming that all firms are passive "price takers." This leads directly to an exclusive emphasis on the elasticity of demand of the market as a whole, which in the case of international trade leads to the well known Marshall-Lerner-Robinson condition as a necessary basis for the improvement in the balance of trade in the face of a depreciation or devaluation of the currency. But from the point of view of a more general theory of competition, the demand switching effect is the most powerful one. Given a sufficient cost advantage, a country can always lower its own prices, thereby expanding exports and contracting imports. It follows that a country with a competitive advantage will generally enjoy rising market shares and persistent trade surpluses, while the opposite will hold for a country at a competitive disadvantage.

Other things (such as government deficits) being equal, a persistent trade deficit will tend to make the economy less liquid and thus put pressure on national interest rates. This may in turn attract short-term capital into the country, thereby *covering up* the structural trade imbalance with international borrowing. But then the structural trade problem is transformed into one of rising international indebtedness.

A nation may resort instead to protection (tariffs, subsidies) and direct intervention in foreign trade (quotas, foreign exchange controls). The limitations of these are well known. More important, unless they are merely to serve to temporarily protect a country while it prepares itself for international competition, the problem will reappear (possibly at a worse level) when such devices are exhausted.

Austerity, which in practice means lowering the real wage and/or increasing the intensity of labor, has been another historical response. This may temporarily improve a country's competitive position, but unless it is tied to a rate of modernization sufficient to narrow the gap between national and international rates of growth of productivity, relative real unit costs will once again begin to rise and the problem will be back. In the meantime, the working population is impoverished, the distribution of income is further skewed toward the wealthy, and social and political stability is undermined. In the third world, the increased relative and absolute wealth of the upper segments of society also tends to increase the relative demand for imported goods and thus worsen the balance of trade deficit.

Except for gifts and grants-in-aid, the other way in which a country can compensate for a persistent balance of trade deficit is by attracting long-term foreign investment. This requires that potential unit costs in the country be relatively low. Abundant natural resources provide one possibility. Relatively low wages, coupled with sufficiently high potential productivity (and favorable political and social conditions) provide another. However, even if long-term foreign investment is sufficient to cover the whole of trade deficit, it will do so only as long as the outflow of repatriated profits and dividends is not greater than the current inflow of net new foreign investments. In itself, this implies a rising level of long-term foreign debt, as long as the underlying trade imbalance remains in place.

Modernization is the only remaining alternative, both in theory and in practice. It is only by raising both the level and the growth rate of productivity that a country can, in the long run, prosper in international trade. This may be done through internal means, through (directed) foreign investment, or with the help of other nations. But it will not happen by itself, through the magic of free trade. On the contrary, precisely because free trade reflects the uneven development of nations, by itself it tends to reproduce and even deepen the very inequalities on which it was founded. It follows that success in the free market requires extensive and intensive social, political, and infrastructural support. While this may seem like heresy to the free marketeers of the world, it is nothing new to those familiar with the actual history and practices of successful capitalist nations.

Summary and Conclusions

The arguments in this paper stand in sharp contrast to those of orthodox theory. International competition is not a great equalizer. Rather, like competition within a nation, it rewards the low-cost producer and punishes high-cost producers, other things being equal.

As a corollary, real exchange rates do not automatically move to balance trade between nations. On the contrary, persistent trade imbalances are normal, since they represent the persistent differences in real unit costs that exist among nations.

There is absolutely no requirement that the opening of free trade increase overall employment in the countries involved. Indeed, it is possible that both countries can suffer job losses. Koechlin et al. (1993, pp. 10–12) anticipate exactly such an outcome in the case of NAFTA: they estimate that imports of U.S. and Canadian corn will drive out small agricultural producers and result in Mexican unemployment of between 200 thousand and 2 million people. In addition, they calculate that investment flows diverted from the United States to Mexico will reduce employment in the United States but raise it in Mexico. The overall effect, in their estimation, is to create net job losses in both countries.

The theory outlined here suggests that the creation of a common market is least disruptive when the participants have similar levels of development, similar unit costs, and similar social and institutional structures. To a large extent, this is true of the European Common Market, and even of the 1989 Free Trade Agreement between Canada and the United States. But it is emphatically not true of NAFTA, since Mexicans' wages are roughly one-eighth of those in the United States, while their productivity levels in modern plants approach those of the United States. Here, the question of capital mobility becomes crucial, for if Mexico can provide the social and infrastructural elements to entice a substantial amount of foreign (including U.S.) capital, then its urban job gains may well be associated with corresponding job losses elsewhere. At the same time, as Koechlin et al. (1993) note, agricultural unemployment, and perhaps even total unemployment, in Mexico could rise. The political potential is quite explosive, as recent events in Chiapas, Mexico, make clear.

Lower unit costs, particularly lower unit labor costs, are the key to absolute cost advantage. This means that low-productivity nations face two options if they are to be competitive. They can try to keep real wages sufficiently low, so as to offset their own technological backwardness. Or they can modernize, thereby raising productivity and even providing room for rising wages. The former option shifts the burden of competitiveness onto the backs of the nation's workers. The latter requires firms to take the initiative (with attendant costs and risks) and provides for the possibility of benefits to both workers and firms (workers share the risks in any case, since business failures are associated with layoffs and job loss). This was the traditional route of German industrialization, which began with higher wages than in England but was able through innovation and technical change to lower productivity and more than offset its higher wages. Japanese industrialization, on the other hand, benefited from both lower wages and rapid technical change. Even Korea and Taiwan, which entered the world market with among the lowest wages in the world, were not able to compete effectively except by rapidly increasing the productivity of labor (Amsden, 1991).

But to successfully implement such a path, it may be first necessary to protect industries that are modernizing so that they have time to prepare for their entry into the world market, while at the same time retraining displaced workers and training new ones for this same eventuality. This is particularly important in the present epoch of high unemployment and slow growth, in which gains on one can come at the expense of the other. In the long run, it may be more important to concentrate on stimulating growth than to rush into opening up free trade zones. All of it would require the most careful planning and coordination within and between nations. None of this can be accomplished by abandoning economic and social policy to the dictates of so-called free trade.

—— 5 ——

Unemployment, Capital, and Unskilled Labor

David Schwartzman

Currently in the United States 12.5 percent of blacks are unemployed, despite the fact that real GDP now exceeds the prerecession level. Adding discouraged workers, the black unemployment rate is 14.5 percent. This national disaster is the result of the decline in the demand for unskilled labor since World War II. In 1951–53 the black unemployment rate was 5.3 percent. Even this lower rate reflected a decline in the demand for unskilled labor. Farm laborers in the South were being displaced by tractors, cotton pickers, combines, and cotton gins, and they were moving to cities in the North in search of jobs.

The black unemployment problem is part of the unskilled unemployment problem. I estimate that 52 percent of employed black males are unskilled, compared to 29 percent of white males (see *Statistical Abstract of the United States 1992*, p. 396, Table 631). The average unemployment rate of unskilled workers rose from 3.9 percent in 1951–53 to 7.6 percent in 1987–89. An explanation of the rise in the unskilled unemployment rate will, therefore, account for part of the rise in black unemployment. This modest goal is not to be sneezed at.

True, the skilled unemployment rate also has risen from 1.7 percent to 3.6 percent. I do not try to analyze the growth of the latter. Perhaps unemployment insurance benefits encourage jobless skilled workers to take more time searching for jobs. In any case, it is the high and rising rate of unskilled unemployment that is the urgent problem.

Unskilled unemployment grew over the postwar years because the cost of unskilled labor rose more than the cost of capital, of skilled labor, and of imports of products of unskilled labor in developing countries. The result was the substitution of capital, skilled labor, and imports for unskilled labor. What we call productivity growth consists largely of the substitution of capital and skilled labor for unskilled labor. Productivity growth has benefited the skilled majority of the population, but it has harmed the unskilled. Not only has it caused unemployment, but it is responsible for part of the increase in the inequality of incomes among the employed. Similarly for imports: the trade liberalization policy pursued by all administrations since World War II, including the present one, has had the effect of dumping the unskilled workers into the vast world ocean of unskilled.

The larger study on which this paper is based (which is still in progress and has the working title *Black Unemployment: Unskilled Unemployment*) analyzes all aspects of the decline in the demand for unskilled labor. Here I discuss only the substitution of capital for unskilled labor.

The Cost of Unskilled Labor and of Capital Goods

Over the postwar period the cost of capital goods fell relative to the cost of unskilled labor. The inflation, which continues, brought real interest rates down relative to real wages, and the prices of plants and equipment also fell relative to wages.

Table 5.1 shows the indexes of real interest rates, real average hourly earnings of manufacturing production workers, and the wage–interest rate ratio by decades since 1900. The real interest rates are calculated as the nominal rates minus the rate of inflation. The index of Moody's Aaa bonds, which are thirty-year bonds, measures the change in nominal interest rates. The GDP implicit deflator is the index of inflation. The most dramatic figure is the one for the decade of the 1950s: 1349. Real wages were over thirteen times as high relative to the cost of financing in the 1950s as in 1929. The indexes for the 1960s and 1970s were not as dramatic, but they show that the relative cost of capital was over four times as high in the 1960s as in 1929. Even after real interest rates increased in the 1980s and the growth of real wages of production workers stopped, the wage–interest rate index was as high as 181.

Inflation generally reduces real interest rates. Lawrence Summers (1983, p. 211) has shown that over the period 1860 to 1980, nominal short-term interest rates did not rise when prices rose. In three of the

Table 5.1

Indexes of Real Wages and Interest Rates and of the Wage/Interest Rate Ratio, by Decades, 1900–89 (1929=100)

	Indexes		
	Wages	Interest Rate	Wage/Interest Rate
1900–09	53	40	134
1910–19	56		–53[a]
1920–29	92	118	78
1930–39	113	104	109
1940–49	149		–71[a]
1950–59	180	13	1,349
1960–69	206	44	466
1970–79	222	23	967
1980–89	228	126	181

Notes and sources: Index of real wages based on average hourly earnings of manufacturing production workers deflated by GNP implicit price deflator for all goods and services. Average hourly earnings in manufacturing from *ERP* 1991, p. 336, and *Historical Statistics*, ser. D–802. GNP implicit price deflator for 1899–1949 from *Historical Statistics*, ser. F1–5, vol. 1, p.224. Other years from *ERP* 1991, p.286. Nominal interest rate: Moody's Aaa bond rate 1919–89 from *ERP* 1991, p. 368, and *Historical Statistics*, ser. X477, vol. 2, p.1003. Series extended by unadjusted index of yields of American railroad bonds, ibid., ser. X476, p.1003. Railroad bond index was consistently lower than the Moody rate for 1919–30, so it was multiplied by 1.04. The real interest rate was computed for each year by subtracting the percentage increase in the price deflator from the nominal interest rate.
[a]Not shown because average real interest rate was negative in this period.

twelve decades when inflation was most rapid the real interest rate was negative.

The inflation, and thus the fall in real interest rates, between 1950 and 1979 was the result of monetary and fiscal policies. The credit crunch imposed by the Federal Reserve in 1979 raised real interest rates back to prewar levels. But, as we have seen, the cost of unskilled labor relative to interest rates remained above that of the 1920s.

The prices of investment goods, including structures, rose less than the wages of unskilled labor over the period 1930–89, as Table 5.2 shows. They rose more than the general price level owing to the relatively slow growth of productivity in construction. However, what matters is that wages rose even more.

Changes in production methods also occur with technological advances, which generally have favored greater capital intensity. And

Table 5.2

Indexes of Average Real Wages, Average Real Prices of Investment Goods, and Their Ratio, by Decades, 1929–87 (1929 = 100)

	Indexes		
	Investment Goods Prices	Wages	Wages/Investment Goods Prices
1930–39	106	113	107
1940–49	112	149	133
1950–59	124	180	145
1960–69	123	206	168
1970–79	123	222	180
1980–89	116	228	197

Notes and sources: Index of real prices of investment goods based on GNP implicit deflator for gross private domestic nonresidential investment deflated by GNP implicit price deflator for all goods and services. GNP implicit price deflator 1930–49 for gross private domestic fixed nonresidential investment from *ERP* 1972, p.198. Later years from *ERP* 1991, p. 290. Series linked at 1958. Index of real wages as in Table 5.1.

capital goods have been substituted for unskilled more than for skilled labor. The review of the relevant econometric literature by Hamermesh and Grant (1979) concludes that unskilled labor is a closer substitute for plant and equipment than skilled labor. Search for new production methods is guided by costs, as Mansfield (1968, p. 63) has shown, and, as we have seen, the cost of unskilled labor has risen more than the cost of capital goods. Moreover, at any time a variety of methods are available for the production of a good, some of which are more capital intensive than others. When unskilled labor becomes relatively more expensive, employers will turn more to capital-intensive production methods.

The Substitution of Capital Goods for Unskilled Labor

Throughout the century the capital stock has grown at a much faster rate than total employment, measured by labor hours. The rates of growth of labor hours in Table 5.3 refer to unskilled and skilled labor together, but capital was substituted more for unskilled labor than for skilled labor. The stock of capital of the private economy grew faster in the postwar period than before the war. The growth rate even in the 1980s, when the real interest rate was high, was above that of any of the prewar decades since 1910.

Table 5.3

Private Domestic Economy: Average Annual Rates of Growth of Labor Hours, Capital, and Capital Per Labor Hour, by Decades, 1900–90

	Labor Hours %	Capital	Capital/Hours %
1900–10	2.4	3.2	0.8
1910–20	0.9	2.5	1.6
1920–30	0.4	2.2	1.8
1930–40	−0.7	−0.9	−0.2
1940–50	1.4	2.5	1.1
1950–60	0.2	3.4	3.1
1960–70	0.9	4.3	3.4
1970–80	1.6	4.0	2.4
1980–90	1.7	3.1	1.4
1950–90	1.5	3.9	2.4

Notes and sources: Estimates for 1900–50 based on J. W. Kendrick, *Productivity Trends* (Princeton, N.J.: Princeton University Press, 1961), pp.334–35; estimates for 1950–90 based on *BLS News Release*, August 29, 1991.

What really matters for productivity growth is not the growth rate of the stock of capital, but the growth rate of the stock of capital per labor hour. Whether it is high or low will have no effect on productivity if the number of labor hours grows proportionally. Capital per labor hour must grow for productivity to increase. In the three decades from 1950 to 1980, the rate of growth of capital per labor hour was much greater than in any of the preceding decades of this century. In the 1950s the economy may have been making up for the small growth of the capital stock in the Depression, and much of the growth in the 1940s was for the manufacture of weapons. But the high growth rate continued in the 1960s and 1970s, long after the Depression and the war. Despite the high real interest rates of the 1980s, the growth rate of the capital stock remained above that of the prewar decades since 1910. The growth rate of the capital stock per labor hour was lower than in the 1910s and the 1920s, but that may have been due to the large growth of the labor force. Part of the growth reflects the increased labor force participation of women.

Evidence of the substitution of capital goods for unskilled labor is provided by the Bureau of Labor Statistics (various years) studies of changes in production methods in a large number of industries. Certain common tendencies stand out. Mechanization has advanced in all the industries, and electronic controls have been widely applied. Fewer laborers are needed to handle materials. Electronic sensors have replaced visual inspection. Robots are performing the repetitive, routine tasks formerly done by assembly-line workers. On the other hand, the new capital goods, especially those incorporating electronic controls, have increased the number of technical and managerial jobs. This evidence indicates that capital was substituted more for unskilled than for skilled labor.

Conclusions Regarding Policies

The fiscal and monetary policies of the first three postwar decades were motivated in part at least by the goal of maintaining a high rate of employment in the face of fluctuations in the level of business activity. The only reservation of economists, who have judged the policies to be successful, has been about the unequal effects of the resulting inflation on different kinds of income and the erosion of savings. The policies had the intended effect of stimulating investment, which may have promoted employment stability. However, the policies have contributed to the long-run rising trend of unskilled unemployment.

Other policies also have contributed. I have referred to the trade liberalization policy, which has raised imports. Exports have also grown, but the exports have added to the demands for capital and for skilled labor. The net effect of the policy on unskilled workers has been to reduce the demand for their labor.

The other major policy that has had this effect has been that promoting higher education. The increase in public funding of colleges and universities has increased the number of professionals, managers, and technicians, which has had the effect of depressing the wages paid to these workers. The cost of skilled labor, adjusted for skill, has also fallen with advances in technology. A skilled worker today knows more, even if he or she has had no more schooling than the skilled worker of an earlier generation.

The policies mentioned were not the only sources of the decline in the demand for unskilled labor. Capital per labor hour would have grown even without the inflationary policies, imports would have grown with the expansion of the manufacturing capacity of developing countries even without trade liberalization, and the number of college and high school graduates would have increased whether or not governments contributed as substantially as they did to the support of educational institutions. But the policies probably turned beneficial, desirable progress into a disaster for unskilled workers.

What about remedies? The present paper shows that the theories underlying proposed remedies are wrong. The administration proposes to limit welfare payments, the theory being that a large part of the problem is due to welfare dependency. However, welfare dependency is the result, not the cause, of the growth of unemployment. The administration also proposes to increase expenditure for training programs. However, to train unemployed workers for unskilled jobs will have no effect as long as the demand for unskilled labor continues to fall. As numerous studies have shown, displaced workers have not benefited significantly from training programs.

The administration should abandon its trade liberalization policy. NAFTA was not a good idea, but there is little that we can do about it now. In the GATT agreement the administration has negotiated the elimination of the quotas and high tariffs protecting unskilled textile and apparel workers under the Multifiber Arrangement (MFA) in exchange for concessions from other countries on intellectual property rights and other matters. Again, the administration is pursuing a policy detrimental to the interests of unskilled workers. Implementation would benefit the majority, but the unskilled minority is large. My own position is that when a substantial part of the population is hurt, a policy should not be implemented, even if it benefits the majority. The usual defense of trade liberalization depends on showing that the beneficiaries would be better off even after compensating displaced workers. But history shows that they will not be compensated. The government should reverse the policy of trade liberalization and increase the protection against imports of goods manufactured by unskilled labor.

A direct employment program is needed. The New Deal provides a useful precedent. The most appropriate precedent currently is the Federal Civil Works Administration (FCWA), which paid wages to unemployed workers that state and local governments put to work. These governments, which are strapped for funds, could employ more workers in hospitals, parks, highway departments, schools, sanitation and sewage departments, and the conservation of natural resources.

6

Wageless Recovery, Wageless Growth?
Prospects for U.S. Workers in the 1990s

David M. Gordon

During 1992 and early 1993, many economic observers in the United States bemoaned a "jobless recovery," worrying about "jobless growth" for the 1990s. The Joint Economic Committee of the U.S. Congress observed (1993a, p. 32), for example: "Job growth has been anemic since March 1991, in sharp contrast to the usual pattern. If the job count had shown the percentage gains typical of the past, we would have millions of additional jobs at this point." "Like commuters peering anxiously down the tracks," a *Business Week* cover story, "Jobs, Jobs, Jobs," further cautioned (1993a, p. 68), "millions of unemployed Americans are waiting for the great job express. But the expected surge of hiring is nowhere in sight, even though business profits are up, output is growing, and the economy is recovering."

Unemployment remains a severe problem in the United States. By the end of 1993 (at the time of writing), more than 8 million workers were unemployed, and the unemployment rate hovered well above 6 percent (U.S. Department of Commerce, 1993).

But unemployment is by no means the most serious problem afflicting the vast majority of U.S. workers and households. A far more crippling hardship has been the devastating decline in real wages among production and nonsupervisory workers—who account for roughly 80 percent of total wage and salary employment—since the early 1970s. We should be worrying about the problems of joblessness, to be sure, but we should worry even more about the earnings squeeze facing scores of millions of U.S. workers. We should be shifting our gaze, in short, to concerns about what one might well call the "wage-less recovery" and the prospects for "wageless growth" in the 1990s.

The first section of this chapter reviews the historical record, comparing the relative importance of rising unemployment and declining wages since the early 1970s. The second turns toward the future, exploring what range of initiatives might transform economic prospects for the 1990s from the bleak landscape of wageless growth to a somewhat more hospitable terrain of at least modest improvements in the living standards of the vast majority of U.S. households.

Comparing the Problems of Unemployment and Declining Earnings

I would argue that there are two principal reasons for placing greater priority on the problem of wages than on the problem of unemployment in the United States. First, the hand-wringing about the "jobless recovery" was probably premature and the dire threat of "jobless growth" overblown. Second, and more important, when we compare the relative importance to U.S. households of the problems of rising unemployment and declining wages, the earnings squeeze emerges as the far more serious burden.

A Productivity Surge?

There have been two principal sources of concern about the jobless recovery and, by extrapolation, jobless growth.

One involves the sluggishness of output growth during the recent recovery: during the first eight quarters of the recent recovery (1991.2–1993.1), nonfarm business output (NIPA measure) grew at an average annual rate of only 2.5 percent, scarcely more than two-fifths of the average over the first eight quarters of the previous seven recoveries in the postwar period (U.S. Department of Commerce, various years). If output growth continues to be sluggish, obviously, then employment growth can hardly be buoyant.

For those concerned about the jobless recovery, however, many felt that output growth might eventually pick up its pace (as indeed, it had at the time of writing in the last two quarters of 1993). Of far greater concern was the appearance of a surge of productivity growth, soaking up almost all of output growth and leaving little or nothing for the growth of employment. "The U.S. economy has changed," the *Business Week* article warned portentously (p. 68), "in ways that have fractured the historic link between output growth and job creation."

Productivity growth during 1992 was indeed rapid—reaching an annual rate of 3.2 percent in the nonfarm business sector (NFB) during the four quarters of that year. For such a "surge" to be lasting, however, it would have to prove to be more than a merely cyclical correction, constituting instead a fundamental acceleration in the underlying trend rate of growth of hourly output.

The postwar pattern of productivity growth over the business cycle has consistently featured slow growth toward the end of expansion and a rapid acceleration—featuring a kind of short-term "correction"—at the beginning of the recovery (R.J. Gordon, 1979). For us to project jobless growth during the 1990s, we would have to be certain that the surge of productivity growth in 1992 represented more than such a short-term correction at the beginning of the recent recovery.

This does not appear to have been the case. The end of the long 1980s expansion witnessed even more than usually sluggish productivity growth, perhaps due to over optimistic hiring decisions after a relatively long period of prosperity. Robert J. Gordon (1993) has made careful efforts to separate longer-term trends from recent cyclical effects and concludes, on balance, that the layoffs and sluggish employment expansion of 1991–92 primarily constituted a short-term correction of that late-expansion over-optimism. He finds that the 1991–92 improvement in productivity growth is entirely consistent with expectations based on past cyclical behavior and that there is very little if any evidence of an increase in the historical trend rate of productivity growth in the United States, which itself has crawled at an average annual rate of less than 1 percent (for the nonfarm business sector) since the early 1970s. He concluded in early 1993:

> If the economic difficulties of the early 1990s come to be labeled generally as an economic hangover, then the jobless recovery of 1991–92 can be viewed as a hangover reaction to a binge of overhiring in the late 1980s—just as sluggish spending by consumers and business firms has come to be viewed widely as a hangover reaction to excess indebtedness incurred in the mid- to late 1980s. Perhaps the business press could be urged to replace the common expression "corporate restructuring" with the more appropriate phrase, "correcting our past mistakes." (p. 306)

I share Robert Gordon's skepticism about the evidence of an acceleration of the underlying trend rate of growth of hourly output in the early 1990s. As of the time of writing this essay, indeed, Gordon's projections were receiving substantial confirmation. During the first three quarters of 1993, after the buoyant 1992 surge, real NFB hourly output remained almost exactly flat; virtually all of output growth was now going toward the generation of employment, and the unemployment rate fell from 7.1 percent in January 1993 to 6.4 percent by the year's end (U.S. Department of Commerce, 1993).

I do not regard an unemployment rate of more than 6 percent as acceptable, and I certainly advocate policy measures that might reduce it substantially. But there appears to be little evidence that the problems of unemployment in the U.S. economy are going to prove any more acute during the 1990s than they were during the late 1970s and 1980s. And compared to problems over that period, the impact of the wage squeeze has been much more severe. It is toward the comparative assessment of the relative severity of those problems that I now turn.

Workers' Employment Earnings Potential

It has always been difficult to "compare" the relative severity of the problems of unemployment and stagnant or declining earnings. Those who are actually jobless could only wish that they were so lucky as to be facing the earnings problems affecting the more numerous employed. And those who enjoy relative job security, even if faced with a wage squeeze, may selfishly savor their "insider" status and care little about the outsiders who figuratively clamor at the factory gates and office elevators. How could one possibly weigh the relative severity of the problems of one group against those of the other?

During the late 1960s and early 1970s, some social scientists addressed this methodological problem by developing various measures of "underemployment." These indices sought to sum together the problems of the jobless, of discouraged workers, of involuntarily part-time employees, *and* of employed workers with "less-than-adequate" or "poverty" earnings. (See D.M. Gordon, 1972, 1977.) While all of these proposed indices suffered from a variety of measurement problems and the arbitrariness of any absolute index of poverty or adequate earnings, they nonetheless seemed relevant for a period of general prosperity in which jobs and earnings problems were primarily limited to those at the bottom of the employment and income distribution.

Times have changed dramatically since then. If we define the "vast majority" of U.S. workers and households as the bottom 80 percent of the income distribution, which is conveniently consistent with the portion of wage-and-salary employees working in "production or non-supervisory" occupations, then the *average* or *median* worker and household in that group—and not merely the less advantaged—has suffered mounting problems of sustaining, much less improving their well-being since the early 1970s. Table 6.1 charts some of the main indicators of this spreading adversity, tracking key economic measures for the business cycle peaks of 1966, 1973, 1979, and 1989—as well as for 1992, the most recent year for which data were available at the time of writing and a year still in the early stages of the recovery. (Here and throughout the rest of this paper, business-cycle peaks are defined as the peak in a series of aggregate capacity utilization, which is in turn defined as the ratio of real output to real potential output. Peaks measured in this way consistently occur before cycle peaks in real output itself. For full definition and documentation of this measure of aggregate capacity utilization, see Bowles, Gordon, and Weisskopf, 1989.)

For this vast majority of workers, two principal trends determine the level of income available to their households: take-home pay per hour of work and total hours worked to support household members.

Row [1] presents data on the rate of change of the average production worker's take-home pay—or *real spendable hourly earnings.* Production and nonsupervisory workers comprised 81 percent of total employment in 1992 (U.S. Bureau of Labor Statistics, 1993) and represent that group in the labor force that is most clearly dependent on wage and salary income. Spendable hourly earnings measure the average worker's hourly wage and/or salary income minus personal income taxes and Social Security taxes. These earnings are expressed in constant dollars in order to adjust for the effects of inflation on the cost of living. This series thus measures the real value of workers' hourly take-home pay.

The data show a clear pattern. The average worker's real after-tax pay reached its postwar peak in the early 1970s and then declined consistently through each successive cycle into the early 1990s. By 1992, workers' take-home pay had fallen 18 percent *below* its postwar peak in 1973.

Table 6.1

Impact of Stagnation on People's Well-Being

	1966	1973	1979	1989	1992
[1] Real spendable hourly earnings (1992$)	9.57	10.37	9.88	9.03	8.80
[2] Annual hours worked per capita	682	707	742	790	755
[3] Real median family income (1992$)	33,065	38,080	37,853	38,712	na
[4] Civilian unemployment rate (%)	3.7	4.9	5.8	5.3	7.4

Sources:

[1] Real after-tax hourly earnings of production and nonsupervisory workers (1992$). T.E. Weisskopf, "Use of Hourly Earnings Proposed to Revise Spendable Earnings Series," *Monthly Labor Review*, 1984, pp.38–42, and annual updates by the present author.

[2] Hours worked divided by population, *National Income and Product Accounts*, Table 6.11:1; *Current Population Reports*, ser. P–25.

[3] Real median family income (1992$), *Current Population Reports*, ser. P–60, no.160, Table 11.

[4] Average annual civilian unemployment rate, *Economic Report of the President*, 1993, Table B–30.

Row [2] presents data on average annual *hours worked per capita* by the U.S. population. This measure reflects the total amount of labor that U.S. households committed to the economy in order to support themselves and their dependents. The data on hours approximately mirror the data on real spendable hourly earnings. Not shown directly in the table, average hours per capita declined fairly steadily from the late 1940s until the early 1960s—as workers and households were able to take advantage of rising wage and salary income. Hours fell from a peak of 704 per year during the Korean War to a postwar low of 627 in 1961.

Average annual hours then began to rise in the mid-1960s when real earnings growth began to slow. As real spendable hourly earnings first stagnated and then absolutely declined, average annual hours increased steadily from each business cycle to the next through the late 1980s. They declined slightly from the peak in 1989 to the early-recovery measure in 1992, reflecting the sluggish recovery of employment from the 1990–91 recession.

This increase in average annual hours per capita reflected an increase in the number of household members working outside the home, and not an increase in average hours per week. Faced with stagnating and then declining real spendable earnings, additional family members, particularly married women, sought work. The percentage of the adult population working or looking for work outside the home—a figure that had been roughly constant over the postwar period—began to rise in the mid-1960s, climbing from 59 percent in 1966 to 66 percent in 1989 (Executive Office of the President, 1993, Table B–32). This extra labor helped sustain total household earnings, making possible continued increases in household consumption levels. (On the "overworked American," see Schor, 1991.)

This shows up quite clearly in data on real median family income (row [3]), a measure of the standard of living that the typical U.S. family could afford as the postwar period progressed. Families could sustain rapidly improving living standards during the decades of prosperity, with real median family income rising at an average annual rate of 3.1 percent in 1948–66 (not shown in table). After the mid-1960s, however, the slowdown in hourly earnings began to take hold, with the rate of growth of real median family income in 1966–73 falling 30 percent below its pace during the boom years. After the early 1970s, finally, stagnation became fully manifest, with real median incomes actually declining slightly from 1973 to 1979 and then barely recovering to 1989. Despite the substantial increases in average hours worked (row [2]) after the early 1970s, the decline in hourly take-home pay (row [1]) was so severe that family incomes could barely keep pace with inflation.

At the same time, problems of unemployment were also increasing. Row [4] tracks the average annual civilian unemployment rate. It rose from the cycle peak of 1966 through the peaks of 1973 and 1979, reflecting the effects of stagflation. It then declined slightly to the peak of 1989, now reflecting the low-wage, rapid-job-growth trajectory of the 1980s expansion. In 1992, after a year of "jobless" recovery, the unemployment rate was still well above 7 percent.

These various indicators tell a clear story about the shift from the boom period to the period of stagnation in the United States. Whereas problems of underemployment used to affect only the most disadvantaged in the labor force, problems of earnings squeeze and overwork have more recently been affecting the *average* worker. We need a new measure, replacing the old concept of underemployment, that addresses the pervasiveness of earnings and employment problems in the United States.

I have devised for these purposes an index of *workers' employment earnings potential*, designed to combine earnings and employment problems in a single measure. It is defined as the ratio of total nonfarm real annual spendable earnings for production-nonsupervisory employees (in 1992$) divided by the total number of workers who would like to share in those earnings. More specifically, the numerator is measured as real spendable hourly earnings times total annual hours worked by production and nonsupervisory employees in the nonfarm sector. The denominator is measured as the sum of the nonfarm civilian labor force and "discouraged workers" adjusted by the ratio of production-nonsupervisory workers to total employment, resulting in a measure of the full potential production-nonsupervisory labor force. The adjustment in the denominator involves the (necessary) assumption that the proportion of the unemployed and discouraged workers who are production or nonsupervisory employees is the same as for those who are employed. We cannot avoid this assumption on the basis of easily available data. In fact, it is undoubtedly the case that the proportion of production-nonsupervisory employees among the unemployed and discouraged workers is greater than for those already employed, which would result in the denominator being larger than I have measured it. But, as long as this bias does not change substantially over time, which seems unlikely, my measure should still provide us with a decent indication of trends in employment earnings potential even if the intercept of the measure should be somewhat lower (because of a higher denominator).

This measure of workers' employment earnings potential thus tracks the average annual take-home pay that workers would enjoy *if* everyone who wants to work were able to share in the available wage-and-salary employment income. The index is an artificial construct, to be sure, notionally premised on the counterfactual idea that total (production-nonsupervisory) employment earnings are available to be shared by all those currently working *and* those who would like to work. But it nonetheless has two distinctly appealing advantages. First, by including the unemployed and discouraged workers in the denominator, it allows us to assess the relative importance of rising joblessness and declining earnings in a composite measure of workers' employment earnings potential. (The more that unemployment rises, for example, the higher will be the denominator and the lower will be the measure of employment earnings potential.) Second, as a corollary, it allows us to conduct some counterfactual thought experiments designed to assess how much relative impact over time both declining earnings and rising unemployment have had on workers' earnings potential.

Figure 6.1 graphs this measure of workers' employment earnings potential (in 1992$) for the U.S. economy from 1948 to 1992. By this construction, workers' annual potential employment earnings rose from roughly $11,500 in 1948 to a postwar peak of almost $18,000 in 1973. Since then it has declined consistently, with obvious cyclical variations. By the cycle peak of 1989, it had fallen to roughly $15,000 and through the early-recovery year of 1992 had declined further to scarcely more than $14,000. By 1992, workers' employment earnings potential had fallen below the levels it had reached in the late 1950s and early 1960s and had dropped more than 20 percent below its 1973 peak.

Still operating at a descriptive statistical level, we can get some sense of what contributed to this sharp decline in earnings potential by conducting a series of counterfactual experiments. Table 6.2 presents the results of these successive exercises for the same years as presented in Table 6.1.

Figure 6.1 **Workers' Employment Earnings Potential** (Real Annual Spendable Earnings Per Potential Employee [1992$]; U.S. Nonfarm Production-Nonsupervisory Employees, 1948–92)

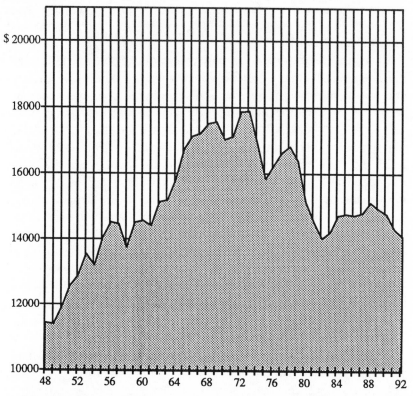

I begin with the problem of rising unemployment. How much of the decline in workers' employment earnings potential since the early 1970s would have been moderated if there had not been the secular rise in unemployment rates accompanying stagflation? For this thought experiment I hold the unemployment rate constant at "full employment" levels—at 4 percent—from 1970 through 1992. Row [2] shows the level of workers' employment earnings potential at "full employment." As is obvious from the table, the operation of the economy at 4 percent unemployment after the 1960s would have made only the most marginal difference in workers' potential earnings. At the greatest, at the business cycle peak of 1979, comparing row [2] with row [1], workers' employment earnings potential would have been only $345 higher per potential employee (in 1992$) under a "full employment" regime.

Table 6.2

Components of Decline in Workers' Employment Earnings Potential
(1992$)

	1966	1973	1979	1989	1992	%
[1] Actual historical values	17,140	17,895	16,389	14,949	14,119	—
[2] At 4% unemployment rate	17,140	18,083	16,734	15,154	14,664	3.3
[3] At 1972 payroll tax rate ceiling	17,140	18,003	16,537	15,294	14,465	1.4
[4] At 1% real wage growth after 1973	17,140	17,895	18,181	19,965	20,054	19.9
[5] Combined effect of rows [2]-[4]	17,140	18,190	18,673	20,515	20,945	24.7

Sources: In the numerator, real spendable hourly earnings are from the source listed for row [1] in Table 1, while annual nonfarm production-nonsupervisory hours are derived by multiplying total annual nonfarm hours (U.S. Department of Commerce, *Business Conditions Digest*, series no. 48, various years) times the ratio of production-nonsupervisory to total employment in the private nonfarm sector (U.S. Bureau of Labor Statistics, 1993, various years). In the denominator, total civilian labor force and agricultural employment are from Executive Office of the President (1993, Table B-30), and "discouraged workers" are defined as those not in the labor force who want a job now but think they cannot find one (from U.S. Bureau of Labor Statistics, 1988, Table B-9; and annual updates in U.S. Bureau of Labor Statistics, 1993, various years). Data on discouraged workers extend backward only to 1970; estimates for earlier years are derived by backward forecast based on the relationship between the unemployment rate and the discouraged worker rate for the years 1970 through 1992. (This extrapolation, while crude and unavoidable, does not affect the main points of my story of an earnings squeeze, which begins in the early 1970s.)

Given that the thought experiment involves holding the unemployment rate constant at 4 percent across the full business cycle, the increase in earnings potential during business-cycle recessions was much greater than at business-cycle peaks. Even with those larger differences during recessions, however, the cumulative impact of this full-employment exercise remains marginal. The final column of the table presents the cumulative percentage increase in workers' employment earnings potential over the 1973–92 period that was attributable to the respective thought experiments—in this case, to the assumption of sustained full employment. Even with the unemployment rate held constant at 4 percent in every year over those two decades, workers' potential earnings would have increased cumulatively by only 3.3 percent over their actual historical levels.

A second, presumably minor source of the decline in workers' employment earnings potential over the past twenty-five years stemmed from the steady increases in U.S. payroll tax rates, rising from a level of 4.20 percent in 1966 to 7.65 percent in 1992. Suppose we counterfactually impose a ceiling on payroll tax rates at their level of 5.2 percent in 1972. Row [3] of Table 6.2 shows the results of this exercise. Here too, the simulated increase in workers' employment earnings potential is small, even smaller than with the full-employment experiment. The largest difference emerges at the peak of 1989, with earnings potential $345 higher, while the cumulative percentage increase with a payroll tax ceiling is only 1.4 percent.

With these thought experiments as a warm-up, it should not be surprising that the major source of the decline in workers' employment earnings potential resulted from the sharp declines in real before-tax hourly earnings for production and nonsupervisory workers. We can dramatize this result with a third exercise. After growing rapidly during the boom period, real wage growth began to slow between 1966 and 1973 before beginning to fall over the next two business cycles. Average annual growth in real spendable hourly earnings in 1966–73 was barely more than 1 percent a year. Suppose that real before-tax hourly earnings had continued to grow at 1 percent a year from 1973 to 1992 instead of actually declining.

We can see in row [4] of Table 6.2 how much difference in total workers' employment earnings potential such a counterfactual difference would have made. Workers' employment earnings potential would have continued to grow after 1973, instead of declining—despite rising payroll tax rates and rising unemployment. By the peak in 1989, average annual earnings potential would have been slightly more than $5,000 higher (in 1992$) than its actual historical value, rising to roughly 12 percent above its 1973 peak instead of falling to more than 20 percent below it. As the last column of row [4] shows, the cumulative increase in workers' employment earnings potential over the full twenty years would have been roughly one-fifth.

Row [5] of Table 6.2 and Figure 6.2 illustrate the combined effect and relative weight of these three exercises. They begin with the actual observed values for workers' employment earnings potential presented in Figure 6.1 and then successively add the results of each of the three counterfactual experiments, involving "full employment," a payroll tax ceiling, and a post-1973 1 percent growth rate in real before-tax hourly

Figure 6.2 **Workers' Employment Earnings Potential with Combined Simulated "Counterfactuals"** (Real Annual Spendable Earnings Per Potential Employee [1992$]; U.S. Nonfarm Spendable Earnings Per Potential Employees, 1948–92)

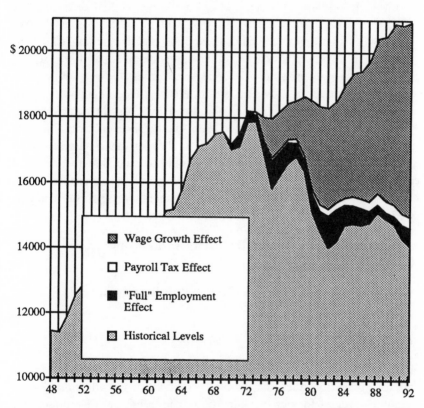

earnings. As the figure shows most graphically, the combined effect succeeds in substantially reversing the post-1973 decline in earnings potential, with the shift from a negative to a small positive growth rate of real hourly earnings accounting for four-fifths of the cumulative combined improvement in workers' potential well-being.

All of this suggests, in short, that if we rely on a welfare measure of potential annual earnings, the quantitatively most important problem afflicting U.S. workers over the past twenty years has resulted from a persistent wage squeeze, not from rising joblessness.

These exercises involve descriptive statistics and decompositional exercises, not explanatory analysis. At the level of explanation, of course, it is likely that rising unemployment contributed substantially to slower wage growth, among many other factors. At the same time, however, it is possible that more sluggish wage growth contributed substantially to rising unemployment—through increased labor supply resulting from stagnating household incomes; potential distributional effects on consumption and investment; feedback effects on productivity growth from diminished labor incentives; and dampening effects on government revenues (and thus, other things being equal, fiscal stimulus) in an era of decreasingly progressive tax rates.

The wage squeeze shows no sign of abating. Real spendable hourly earnings have continued to fall (slightly) even as the recovery has picked up. Their level in October 1993, the most recent available data at the time of writing, fell slightly below that for 1992, represented in row [1] of Table 6.1. If these trends continue, we should indeed be worrying more about a wageless recovery and wageless growth in the 1990s than about the problem of unemployment by itself. But worry as we might, can anything be done about the wage squeeze?

Are Rising Real Wages and Reduced Unemployment Compatible?

What would it take to improve workers' well-being in the U.S. economy in the 1990s?

The Crucial Role of Productivity Growth

If the wage squeeze has been as important as I have suggested in the preceding section, then the pace of productivity growth immediately becomes crucial for our consideration. The trend rate of productivity growth in the U.S. nonfarm business sector has been slightly less than 1 percent since the 1970s. This imposes a sharp constraint on real wage growth. For real wage growth to rise above that level, much less even to approach it, would begin to expose the economy to a number of crippling burdens. Real wage growth faster than productivity growth would reduce the profit share over time and potentially dampen investment as a result. Real wage growth faster than productivity growth would also, by definition, increase real unit labor costs, which, in a competitive global economy with flexible exchange rates, would tend further to erode the competitive position of U.S. corporations, eroding net exports. With both investment and net exports suffering, output growth itself would presumably suffer.

An alternative scenario of "wage-led growth" can be constructed according to which rapid real wage growth stimulates consumption, and demand pressures further stimulate investment. While this scenario has a certain appeal, the empirical evidence does not seem to support it as a likely construction for the United States or many other advanced economies (see D.M. Gordon, 1995; S. Bowles and R. Boyer, 1995).

In the United States, NFB productivity growth raced at an average annual rate of 2.6 percent during the long boom from 1948 to 1966 (Bowles, Gordon, and Weisskopf, 1990, Table 10.1). Since the 1970s, it has been limping at a trend rate of growth of below 1.0 percent (R.J. Gordon, 1993). I do not believe that the trend productivity growth rate in the U.S. economy could be realistically expected to rebound quickly to anything like its pace during the postwar boom. But there is considerable space between 1.0 percent and 2.6 percent, and it is not unreasonable to expect that the trend rate could be improved beyond its recent levels.

This is not an essay directly about productivity growth itself. I and my colleagues have written at length elsewhere (for example, in D.M. Gordon, 1995; and in Bowles, Gordon, and Weisskopf, 1990, chapters 11–14) about the requirements and possibilities for substantial improvements in the rate of growth of productivity in the United States in the medium term. Relying on that work, I shall presume here that a combination of sustained fiscal and monetary support of private investment, expanded public investments in infrastructure and training, improved opportunities for worker protection and worker "voice" in production, and credit market support for democratic enterprises could potentially increase the trend rate of productivity growth *even without substantial increases in the recent trend rate of aggregate output growth.*

How much of an increase in the trend rate of productivity growth could be achieved? Future gazing is inherently speculative and unreliable, especially when it draws upon presumptions of important policy and structural changes, which are themselves difficult to forecast. For the purposes of the discussion that follows, however, let us suppose that a combination of feasible policy changes could make up half the difference between the productivity growth rates of the postwar boom and the recent period of sluggish improvement. Let us imagine, therefore, that a trend rate of productivity growth in the late 1990s of 1.8 percent a year is plausible, at least for the purposes of discussion, under a more favorable policy regime.

But productivity growth is crucial for our discussion for more reasons than its creating room for enhanced real wage growth. At given rates of output growth, more rapid productivity growth will diminish the growth of employment and compound problems of unemployment. Those who have been primarily concerned about problems of joblessness, indeed, have often been wary of accelerated productivity growth for precisely this reason.

There is a severe risk in the U.S. economy of continuing wageless growth in the 1990s. Enhanced productivity growth is essential to the possibilities of ameliorating this prospect. But is it possible that accelerated productivity growth and real wage growth can be accomplished without reviving fears of jobless growth?

Alternative Growth Paths

I explore in this section the *consistency* of improved wage growth and moderated unemployment for the U.S. economy in the 1990s. I concentrate here not on the probabilities of major shifts in U.S. economic policy, but more narrowly on the formal logical possibility of achieving a medium-term growth path that would unequivocally improve workers' well-being.

For such an exercise we need to resort to a number of accounting identities that constrain the crucial growth relationships in which we are interested. Four are most salient for our purposes here, with all money flows denominated in real terms.

- Output growth is distributed between growth in labor hours and growth in hourly output. Given a rate of growth of output, an increase in productivity growth must necessarily diminish the growth of the labor hours necessary to produce that output.
- Productivity growth can itself be viewed as distributed between hourly wage growth for production workers and the growth of gross hourly surplus, which in turn includes hourly wages for nonproduction employees, unit interest costs, and unit net profits. At a given rate of productivity growth, an increase in hourly wage growth would require that something else give way, such as interest payments or net profits.
- Growth in labor demand, measured in hours, is in turn divided between growth in employment—in the number of jobs—and growth in average annual hours worked. For example, if average annual

Table 6.3

What Happens to Output Growth? An Exercise in Growth Accounting

	Boom 1948.2– 1966.1	1980s 1978.4– 1989.2	1990s Scenario No. 1	1990s Scenario No. 2
[1] % real NFB output growth	4.19	2.76	3.0	3.0
[2] % real NFB productivity growth	2.93	1.14	1.1	1.8
[3] % real hourly wage growth	2.14	−0.24	0.0	1.0
[4] % gross unit surplus growth	0.80	1.38	1.0	0.8
[5] % real production-nonsup. hours	1.26	1.62	1.9	1.2
[6] % production-nonsup. employment	1.24	1.82	1.9	1.6
[7] % average annual hrs growth	0.02	−0.20	0.0	−0.4
[8] % change civilian labor force (16+)	1.21	1.70	1.7	1.4

Sources: Data for the historical parts of the exercise come from standard data provided by the U.S. Bureau of Labor Statistics in various sources. The output measure is the BLS measure of NFB output. The determination of productivity, wages, hours, and employment for production-nonsupervisory workers is accomplished by assuming that the employment proportions and production-worker wage levels in the NFB sector are the same as for the private nonfarm sector.

hours worked declines—perhaps as a result of a reduced working week—then the rate of growth of jobs could be more rapid than the rate of growth of hours.

• All of this must be benchmarked against the average annual rate of growth of labor supply. If the rate of growth of jobs is more rapid than the rate of growth of the labor force, for example, then the unemployment rate will decline.

Table 6.3 explores the interrelationships among these crucial growth rates, both for actual historical experiences in the postwar U.S. economy and for two alternative hypothetical scenarios for the 1990s. The table focuses exclusively on the nonfarm business sector, NFB, ignoring for the purposes of discussion whatever compensating or reinforcing effects may flow from direct government activity.

From the vantage point of workers, one would hope for a growth regime that fostered both rapid real wage growth and low or declining unemployment. But one could easily imagine three alternative possibilities: (a) a rapid wage-growth regime with high or rising unemployment; (b) a rapid job-growth regime with stagnant or declining real wages; or (c) an especially inhospitable trajectory with stagnant or declining real wages and high or rising unemployment.

The Golden Age

The first column of Table 6.3 displays the key growth rates for the U.S. economy during the long postwar boom from 1948 to 1966. NFB output growth was rapid (row [1]), accompanied and to some extent stimulated by an unusually rapid rate of productivity growth (row [2]).

On the employment side, this allowed for a reasonably rapid growth in labor hours (row [5]). Because average annual hours remained flat (row [7]), employment growth (row [6]) occurred at the same pace as hours, resulting in a job-growth rate that turned out to be almost exactly equal to the rate of growth of the civilian labor force. Unemployment was already quite low in the immediate postwar years (resting at 3.8 percent in 1948), so unemployment remained low at the end of the boom as well.

And there was plenty of room for rapid real wage growth as well. With productivity growth so rapid, real wages were able to increase at more than 2 percent a year (row [3]) while still leaving a healthy margin of growth in gross unit surplus (row [4]) to allow, *inter alia*, for sustained investment financed at least partly out of retained earnings.

This was the arithmetic of the Golden Age: workers enjoyed both rapid real wage growth and low unemployment, while the economy rode the waves of rapid productivity growth and sustained investment.

The Right-Wing Policy Regime

In the 1980s, by contrast, the growth arithmetic had changed dramatically—as the second column of Table 6.3 shows. (I skip over the two intervening business cycles in order to heighten the contrast between the boom years and the eighties.)

First, as was true across the advanced economies, NFB output growth slowed dramatically (row [1]) in comparison to the boom. Productivity growth remained sluggish (row [2]), which meant that a relatively high proportion of output growth resulted in growth in labor demand (row [5]). The rate of growth of labor hours during the 1980s, indeed, was even more rapid than during the long boom.

As a result of this rapid growth in hours, amplified in part by a slight decline in average annual hours worked (row [7]), job growth was especially rapid during the 1980s—as the supporters of right-wing economic policy frequently reminded us. Indeed, even though the rate of growth of labor supply was more rapid during the 1980s than during the boom period (row [8]) (at least partly as a result of households' efforts to offset the wage squeeze), job growth was just barely rapid enough to allow a slight decrease in unemployment (from 5.9 percent in 1979 to 5.3 percent in 1989).

As already indicated, real wage growth was negative during the 1980s (row [3]). Even though hourly output growth remained sluggish, declining real wages were consistent with a dramatic increase in gross unit surplus, increasing at an average annual rate of 1.5 percent (row [4]). This was, indeed, the distributional leitmotif of right-wing economics, with the increases in gross unit surplus distributed handsomely among wage-and-salary income for nonproduction-supervisory employees (especially those near the top of the corporate pyramid), interest payments (enriching the financial sector), and before-tax profits.

The reader might wonder whether some of the decline in workers' real hourly wages was offset by an increase in employee benefits paid by corporations—which would appear in the table not in row [3] for wage growth but rather as part of the growth in gross unit surplus in row [4]. In fact, however, according to the underlying National Income and Product Account data, employee wage supplements paid by corporations (defined as the difference between wage-and-salary compensation and wage-and-salary earnings) remained almost exactly flat during the 1980s—with benefit "givebacks" apparently offsetting increases in health-care costs.

The 1980s thus featured a growth trajectory resembling possibility (b) above, with rapid job growth and stagnant or declining real hourly earnings. In this respect, the U.S. experience contrasted with that of many European economies during the 1980s, where sustained real wage growth was combined with high or rising unemployment, possibility (a) above.

What can we expect during the 1990s?

The 1990s—Scenario No. 1

If early 1990s economic policy and the early performance of the recovery can provide us any guide, we are likely to experience a growth scenario strikingly similar to that of the 1980s. (On the logic of the new policy regime under the Clinton administration, see D.M. Gordon, 1993.) The third column in Table 6.3 outlines this possibility.

I assume that NFB output growth will continue more or less at the same rate as during the 1980s and during the first two years of the recovery, at roughly 3.0 percent a year (row [1]). I also assume that productivity growth continues at its historical trend over the past fifteen years, at roughly 1.1 percent a year (row [2]). (This is consistent with the evaluation by R.J. Gordon, 1993, of the first years of the recovery.) On the *optimistic* assumption that under the current policy regime wage decline might eventually be halted, I assume flat real hourly wages (row [3]), leaving a healthy (though slightly reduced) rate of increase in gross unit surplus (row [4]) for nonproduction-supervisory employees, financial interests, and profit income.

Under these assumptions, rapid job growth would be able to continue, with hours demand increasing at 1.9 percent a year (row [5]). Assuming that average annual hours growth flattens out (row [7]), at least partly because workers will push to sustain hours in order to offset two decades of the earnings squeeze, job growth would be even more rapid than during the 1980s. On the assumption that labor supply growth remains roughly the same as during the 1980s cycle, this rapid job growth would permit further (marginal) decline in the unemployment rate—eventually pushing it below 5 percent at the next business cycle peak.

Though marginally different in the particulars, this growth scenario shares the same basic contours as the 1980s cycle. Under that hypothetical trajectory, the U.S. economy would continue to travel steadfastly along a track featuring rapid job growth with stagnant or declining earnings. Given my analysis of the first main section of this essay, such a scenario would provide little hope to the vast majority of U.S. workers of even modest improvements in their well-being.

The 1990s—Scenario No. 2

Could we hope for better? I outline here the internal logic of an alternative growth scenario for the 1990s that would afford U.S. workers relief from the austerity to which they have been subjected for the past fifteen years—presented in the fourth column of Table 6.3.

In order to focus the comparison between the two growth narratives as precisely as possible, I begin by assuming the same rate of growth of NFB output as for Scenario no. 1. I believe that the kind of growth path I sketch here could eventually lead to more rapid output growth as well, but I would prefer to set that possibility aside in order to concentrate on the distribution of the proceeds of a given output growth rate.

I then assume an intersecting combination of structural changes in economic behavior and economic policy affecting three key variables: productivity growth, wage growth, and average annual hours worked.

- As anticipated above, I assume that a combination of changes in private-sector practice and public-sector policy could induce substantial but not monumental improvements in the trend rate of productivity growth. I assume movement toward greater fiscal and monetary support of private investment, expanded public investments in infrastructure and training, improved opportunities for worker protection and worker voice in production, and credit market support for democratic enterprises (see Bowles, Gordon and Weisskopf, 1990, chapters 11–14). I assume that this shift could increase the trend rate of productivity growth from 1.1 percent to 1.8 percent (row [2]).

- I further assume an overlapping set of changes in corporate behavior and public policy that would substantially increase the rate of growth of hourly earnings. I assume changes in labor law that would both increase the likelihood that workers seeking to form unions could realize their ambitions and enhance workers' bargaining power in unionized situations; as well as a substantial increase in the real value of the minimum wage (see Bowles, Gordon, and Weisskopf, 1990, chapters 11–14). As a result of these changes and the greater room for maneuvering afforded by the acceleration of the trend productivity growth rate, I presume that the real wage growth rate could increase from zero to 1 percent a year (row [3])— still far below the pace of the boom period but rapid enough to reverse substantially the trends of the past two decades.

- Finally, I assume a variety of measures aimed at promoting reduced working time and increased work sharing, including health-care reforms that would reduce employers' current disincentive to hire part-time workers and expanded child-care services that would enhance workers' and firms' flexibility in determining working hours (see Schor, 1991). I also assume that the resumption of a positive rate of real wage growth would provide workers with some room and incentive for seeking increased leisure time. As a result, I imagine that the rate of change of average annual hours could drop from 0.0 percent to –0.4 percent (row [7])—a large change but not entirely without precedent. (The rate of change of average annual hours in the 1966.1–1973.1 business cycle, not shown in Table 6.3, was –0.82 percent a year.)

These three shifts in practice and policy are sufficient to sketch a substantially different kind of growth path. With productivity growth up to 1.8 percent (row [2]), growth in hours demanded is slower than in Scenario no. 1—at 1.2 percent a year (row [5]). But the fruits of reduced average annual hours are now harvested, permitting a growth in employment of 1.6 percent a year (row [6]). As a result of the resumption of a positive rate of real wage growth, reducing the pressure on households to expand their labor supplied, I assume that the rate of growth of labor supply drops from 1.7 percent in Scenario no. 1 to 1.4 percent in Scenario no. 2 (row [8]). The combination of jobs growth and labor supply increase would then be consistent with as rapid a reduction in unemployment as had characterized Scenario no. 1.

Even with accelerated real wage growth (row [3]), finally, there would be enough of a differential between productivity growth and real wage growth to afford a decent rate of increase in gross unit surplus of 0.8 percent a year (row [4])—substantially below the engorgements of the 1980s but equivalent to the pace of the boom years, which itself was more than ample to sustain a rapid pace of productive investment.

Taken together, the arithmetic of Scenario no. 2 affords a much more hopeful picture for workers in the United States than Scenario no. 1, charting a growth path that would combine real wage growth with low or declining unemployment. In this it shares much of the basic logic and distributional proportions of the Golden Age—simply on a more modest scale because of the substantial barriers to achieving anything like the combination of rapid output growth and buoyant productivity growth that characterized the boom years.

I have no illusions about the ease of achieving in the United States the kinds of institutional and policy changes that would be necessary to shift from the likelier Scenario no. 1 to the logically plausible Scenario no. 2. But at least such a growth path, providing improved prospects for U.S. workers, is logically possible. Its accounting arithmetic helps clarify which combinations of institutional and policy changes we need to pursue in order to begin shaking off the austerity of the past two decades. (On the possible barriers to and strategies necessary for such changes, see Bowles, Gordon, and Weisskopf, 1990, chapter 14.) The earnings squeeze has been the most serious problem affecting U.S. workers since the early 1970s and is likely to continue as such during the 1990s. We should place the highest possible priority on efforts to reverse that earnings squeeze in our policy analysis and politics in the coming years.

7

Stagnation, Volatility, and the Changing Composition of Aggregate Demand

Edward Nell

By general consensus, the U.S. economy, and indeed, the world economy, worked pretty well during the 1950s and 1960s, but since the early 1970s, it has failed to run smoothly. Nearly everyone agrees that something went wrong. There is no agreement at all, however, on what went wrong, who or what is to blame, or how to fix it. Policies that appeared to work for decades began to fail. In particular, unemployment and inflation, which had always moved in opposite directions, so that inflation could be reduced by allowing unemployment to rise, now appeared to rise and fall together. Both unemployment and inflation rose to unprecedented heights, while overall growth slowed and productivity growth almost ceased.

Thinking in terms of transformational growth (Nell, 1992) may help to put this in perspective. Prior to 1914 (when the foundations of modern economics were developed) it can be argued that the price mechanism operated in ways that tended to stabilize the economy, for small shocks, at any rate—and even today residual elements of this mechanism can be found in some sectors. But the development of the technology of mass production changed the core of the system fundamentally. The postwar economy, based on mass production and the modern corporation, is inherently unstable. Small fluctuations in output and employment are magnified by some variant of the "multiplier-accelerator" mechanism. Prices are, for the most part, flexible only upwards, and the pressures causing inflation are in general not stabilizing. The traditional "price mechanism" in which supply and demand adapt to one another in a stable process, is simply not to be found.

Instead, prices stay constant or drift upward, in a process often largely independent of the pressure of demand, while output and employment adapt to the level of sales in a destabilizing manner—as when the successive spending rounds of the multiplier interact with the accelerator inducement to invest, or in its modified form, the capital-stock adjustment mechanism.

It is difficult to see how such an economy can be stabilized except by a large government sector, whose expenditures move in a countercyclical fashion—the so-called fiscal "automatic stabilizers" instituted after the Second World War. These automatic effects may, however, not be sufficient, and may need to be supplemented by active policy.

It has also been argued that the monetary system provides a stabilizing influence. When output expands, the transactions demand will drive up interest rates, causing investment to contract, and vice versa when output falls. Empirically, the suggested relationships are weak or nonexistent. Theoretically, both connections are flawed: output variations will not affect interest rates if the money required for circulation—the transactions demand—is supplied endogenously by the banking system, and, in any case, a rise in interest rates would not affect investment if the higher level of activity is also raising the profitability of investment.

An alternative explanation to the slow growth and instability of the 1970s and 1980s, the monetarist view, is widely held among professional economists. The failure of demand management is explained by the proposition that markets learned to anticipate and offset the effects of government policies. Thus the Keynesian measures of the early postwar period had, at best, a limited run; once markets caught on to what was happening, the policies stopped being effective. For example, expanding the money supply might have the temporary effect of lowering real wages and thus raising employment—i.e., reducing unemployment. But once money wages caught up, unemployment would rise again to its "natural level," and the only permanent effect of the policy intervention would be the higher price level.

One of the consequences of monetarism, and the new classical doctrines that followed it, is that governments have become less activist. In both the United States and the UK, the weakest upswing of the postwar era is now taking place, and both governments, far from assisting it, are actively pursuing a fiscal policy of austerity, and taking only a moderately expansive monetary stance.

Table 7.1

The Golden Age and the Iron Age

	1948–1969	1970–1991
Unemployment	4.67%	6.69%
Inflation	3.09%	5.75%
Capacity utilization	84.00%	80.00%
GNP growth	3.80%	2.50%
Productivity growth	3.09%	1.34%

Source: Citibase 1994.

The Two Periods of the Postwar Era

We can call the two periods of the postwar era the Golden Age and the Iron Age respectively. The first lasted from the end of the war, or, more precisely, the end of the demobilization period, to the beginning of the 1970s. The second ran from the beginning of the 1970s to the present. In the first, growth was strong, inflation and unemployment both were low, and policy measures generally seemed to work. In the second, by comparison, growth was weak, inflation and unemployment both were high, and policies often failed and even sometimes seemed perversely to make things worse. We can present the contrast in Table 7.1; the numbers are simple averages of the yearly figures.

Unemployment rates in the second period averaged more than one and a half times higher than in the first period. Worse, two kinds of errors affected the later period more seriously than the early period: both the numbers of "discouraged workers," who drop out of the labor force and are thus not counted as unemployed, and underemployment errors (part-time and temporary work counted improperly as full-time) increased substantially in the 1980s.

The increase in idle resources in the second period is confirmed by the Federal Reserve Board's measure of capacity utilization; the average rate in the second period is four points below that of the first. Far from pressing on resources in the second period, as advocates of "crowding out" would have it, demand is clearly insufficient to employ the resources available.

As might be expected when there is a substantial pool of idle resources, the average rate of GNP growth in the second period fell to about 60 percent of its former rate.

The performance of the rate of productivity growth in the second period was even worse: measured as business sector output per employee hour, it fell to about 40 percent of its average rate in the first period. Inflation, on the other hand, surged, despite the absence of demand pressure. Measured as the annual percentage change in the GNP price deflator, its average rate in the second period was 60 percent higher than in the first period. In general, then, the picture is one of sluggish markets and stronger cost inflation.

A more detailed examination confirms this picture. The unemployment rates of men and women follow the upward trend of the general unemployment up to the late 1970s. In the 1980s the women's unemployment rate, which had been typically higher than the rate for men, coincides with the male rate. Or to put it another way, the male rate rises to coincide with the female, perhaps a result of the increasing unemployment rate among adult males. But the most striking feature is the changing pattern of unemployment: after reaching a low in 1968 matched only by 1952, it rises for a decade and a half, exhibiting fluctuations of a significantly greater amplitude. This changed pattern is also seen in the unemployment figures for blue-collar workers, service workers, and white-collar workers.

The historical record of productivity growth, as calculated by the Council of Economic Advisers, is shown in Figure 7.1. This confirms our calculation, although it finds an even more disappointing performance in the second period (partly because the calculation stops earlier). Part of the explanation of the slowdown in productivity growth can be found in the pattern of investment: the stock of capital per production worker grew at an average rate of 2.2 percent in the first period but fell to an average rate of 1.35 percent in the second (Schwartzman, this volume). The OECD *Economic Survey* of the United States finds that productivity growth in manufacturing output flattened during the 1970s, but was otherwise quite strong both before and after. By contrast, nonmanufacturing productivity growth flattened at the end of the 1960s and has remained flat (OECD, pp. 55–57 and 66–67).

An important consequence of slower productivity growth is slower growth in real wages, which stagnated in the 1970s and 1980s. Together with the rise in unemployment, the greater job insecurity due to wider fluctuations, and the changing job mix, this has led to a significant change in the distribution of earnings. The dispersion of money

Figure 7.1 **Historical Growth in Labor Productivity**

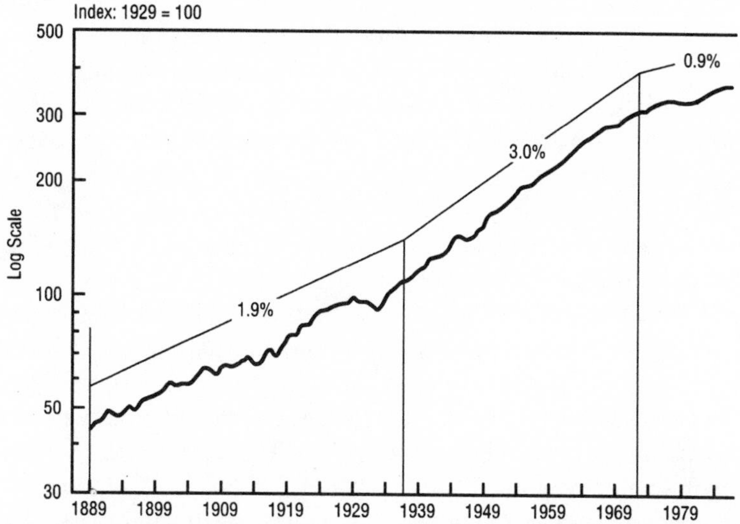

Index: 1929 = 100

Note: Labor productivity has increased steadily over the past century. Productivity has slowed in recent years.

incomes (as measured by the Gini coefficient) declined up to the end of the 1960s but has risen since. That is, the income distribution tended to become more equal in the first period and has tended toward greater inequality during the second. This can be seen in another way by looking at the ratio of earnings for college-educated compared to high-school educated workers; the earnings premium for a college education has increased since the late 1970s. Finally, poverty, which on all standard measures fell rapidly during the 1960s, fell more slowly and uncertainly in the 1970s, rose sharply in the early 1980s, fell a little, and then turned up again in the late 1980s.

These changes are likely to have major effects on consumption and the growth of consumer demand, for they imply that household earning power is more likely to fluctuate and less certain to recover from a setback.

A Political Digression

My central claim is that demand growth has slowed significantly, for a number of reasons, and that to restore prosperity will require an activist expansionary policy. So it is worth asking whether there appear to be any significant differences between the records of the two political parties. In general, Democratic administrations have favored expansionary policies—although the Carter administration, especially in its last two years, retreated from this position. Republican administrations have normally favored policies leaning towards austerity and control of inflation—although Nixon adopted Keynesian expansionist measures before the election of 1972 and Reagan sharply expanded military spending while permitting large deficits. However, both Nixon and Reagan supported deregulation, cutting government social spending, and maintaining high interest rates and tight money.

Table 7.2 compares the economic performance of three Democratic administrations, Truman, Kennedy-Johnson, and Carter, to that of Eisenhower, Nixon-Ford, and Reagan-Bush. The three Democratic periods compared here lasted five, eight, and four years, respectively; the three Republican eight, eight, and eleven. This comparison is quite striking in several respects.

First, taking averages (weighted by the numbers of years), the Democrats outperform the Republicans in all four categories! The contrast is most marked in productivity growth and GNP growth. A striking weakness of the Republican record shows up in productivity growth. The strong record in productivity growth in the earlier period is built up during the Democratic administrations. The weighted average of the Democratic years gives a rate of 2.98 percent. The average Republican productivity growth rate comes out at 1.70 percent. In spite of the dismal record of the Carter years, the overall Democratic performance is two times better than the Republican record. The GNP growth picture is almost as extreme. The Democrats average 4.67 percent, the Republicans, 2.33 percent. Unemployment for the Democrats averages 5.47 percent, for the Republicans, 6.11 percent, closer than might have been expected. Somewhat surprisingly, even on inflation the Republican record over the postwar era is noticeably poorer than that of the Democrats. The weighted average of inflation rates for the Democrats is 4.09 percent, for the Republicans, 4.34 percent.

Second, the weakest Democratic performance comes in the Carter years. But comparing Carter to Nixon-Ford and Reagan-Bush is quite interesting. Carter's unemployment rate is close to Nixon-Ford's and lower than Reagan-Bush's, and his GNP growth rate is higher than either. The disasters are in productivity growth and inflation.

Third, the strong performance of the Golden Age is largely concen-

Table 7.2

The Economic Records of Democrats and Republicans

Unemployment %

Democrats:			Republicans:		
	1948–52	4.26		1953–60	4.89
	1961–68	4.84		1969–76	5.84
	1977–80	6.54		1981–91	7.10
	1992–93	6.81			
	mean	5.47		mean	6.11

Inflation %

Democrats:			Republicans:		
	1948–52	2.92		1953–60	2.40
	1961–68	2.50		1969–76	6.44
	1977–80	8.20		1981–91	4.24
	1992–93	2.21			
	mean	4.09		mean	4.34

Productivity Growth %

Democrats:			Republicans:		
	1948–52	4.32		1953–60	2.55
	1961–68	3.32		1969–76	1.36
	1977–80	0.26		1981–91	1.37
	1992–93	1.38			
	mean	2.98		mean	1.70

GDP Growth %

Democrats:			Republicans:		
	1948–52	5.14		1953–60	3.20
	1961–68	4.75		1969–76	2.41
	1977–80	2.82		1981–91	2.33
	1992–93	2.78			
	mean	4.67		mean	2.33

Source: Citibase.

trated in the Truman and Kennedy-Johnson years. True, the Eisenhower record is the best of the Republicans', but it has a lower GNP growth rate than Carter's, the weakest of the Democrats. The Eisenhower record is weaker than the administrations that preceded and followed it in every category except inflation, where the differences are marginal.

In general, then, it seems that the more expansionist party had the better economic record. Of course, it could be argued that the Korean and Vietnam wars may have helped to make the difference. Yet it is not so obvious that wars could explain the differences. Vietnam contributed nothing to the booming years of 1960–65 and lasted through most of Nixon's period. Also, Reagan boosted defense spending, and Bush had the Gulf War. Furthermore, the Kennedy-Johnson period had the lowest inflation rate, not something war would help.

The data suggest quite simply that policy matters. Other things also matter, of course, but the evidence in the table is consistent with the unfashionable claim that an expansionist policy will tend to lead to higher growth, lower unemployment, and, very likely, a better performance all around.

Reasons for Austerity

Given this record, it is all the more surprising that austerity should be the policy favored not only by conservative governments, but by the general consensus. We have seen socialist austerity in Europe. In the UK, even before Margaret Thatcher, James Callaghan's Labour government, despairing of demand management, set about cutting spending. In the United States, the Clinton administration, like Carter's, toyed with an expansionist policy but then embraced budget cutting. Such a widespread agreement requires some explanation.

There are two closely related ideas that lead governments to adopt an austerity program. The first concerns inflation after the breakdown of the Bretton Woods system. Expansion tends to raise imports, which, with given exports, weakens the currency. In a regime of flexible exchange rates this will tend to put downward pressure on the exchange rate, which raises the costs of imports. This, in turn, sets off a round of price increases. So the party adopting an expansionist program tends to look irresponsible. Everyone suffers from the inflation, and politically, controlling it has come to be seen as the primary objective. Reducing unemployment, by contrast, tends to be seen as favoring labor, even certain segments of labor, rather than the general public. The fact that unemployment means foregone output and slower growth has simply been lost to sight.

The second point concerns the way countries interact. After the breakdown of Bretton Woods, countries faced more serious balance of payments problems. A trade deficit could set off a run against a currency; even the dollar could be subjected to this, as it was in 1979. Furthermore, speculative trading in currencies rose enormously, from about 5 percent in 1970 to become the vast majority of all transactions, as much as 95 percent, twenty years later (Eatwell, this volume). With such great volume, swings in currency values could be hard to contain.

Under these conditions, if a country expanded and its major trading

Table 7.3

The International "Prisoners' Dilemma"

		Trading Partners			
		Austerity		Expansion	
Country A	Austerity	0	0	G	⊣
	Expansion	−L	g	g	g

partners adopted austerity, the country could be in trouble. Its imports would rise at a time when its exports were weak; and short-term capital would flow out because of low domestic interest rates compared to those abroad. These would combine to create a balance of payments crisis, which would drive down the exchange rate. But the immediate impact of this would be to worsen the crisis by reducing earnings from exports. Consider the situation outlined in Table 7.3.

If country A expands and its trading partners do not, it suffers a major loss while they make a small gain. If they also expand, both parties gain. If the partners adopt austerity, neither loses. If A adopts austerity and the trading partners expand, A gains substantially—short-term capital flows in, while exports are strong and imports modest. The effect will be to stimulate the economy through exports, while keeping money tight. Hence, for country A austerity will be the preferred policy. This will apply in succession to every country.

This is a case of the "prisoner's dilemma." The best outcome would be for both parties to expand, but since they must act independently, they are forced to choose defensively, and the best strategy for each will be austerity. Hence, the overall outcome will be inferior.

The Components of Aggregate Demand

As we shall see, part of the explanation of today's Iron Age is that the leading countries systematically followed austerity policies. But this was not the whole story.

Any macro textbook will explain that aggregate demand consists of $C + I + G + (X - M)$; that is, total consumption, plus investment, plus government expenditure, plus net exports. In turn, each of these consists of an "autonomous" component plus an induced component—

Figure 7.2 **Personal Consumption Expenditures** (Durables, Nondurables, Services—Percentage of GNP)

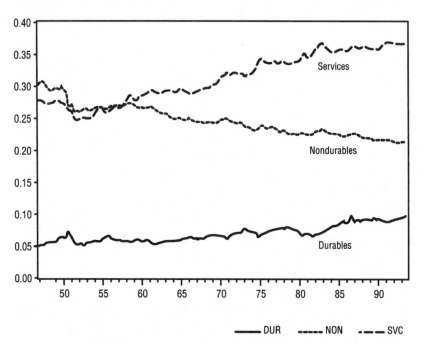

autonomous, that is, in the sense that such expenditures do not depend on the variables of the macroeconomic short run—GNP and interest rates—whereas the induced expenditures do. This point will become important, for it will emerge that there may be a vicious circle of stagnation, created by interaction among the major elements of aggregate demand, which developed only in the later period, following the impact of the oil shock.

Let us consider the elements of aggregate demand in turn:

Consumption

Over the whole postwar era, household consumption grew at about the same pace as GNP; the growth of both series slowed down together in the second period. However, the components of household consumption—durables, nondurables, and services—did not all behave in the same way (see Figure 7.2).

Throughout the period, services rise a little faster than GNP, while nondurables rise much more slowly, falling as a percentage of GNP and thus exerting a downward drag on overall demand. As might be expected, durables fluctuate the most, except during the decade of the 1960s, when they grow strongly at a more rapid rate than GNP. They stagnate again during the 1970s, then grow rapidly in the mid-1980s before flattening out again. The behavior of durables may thus contribute to market uncertainty.

Among nondurables, clothing and the miscellaneous category "other" remained flat; gas first rose a little, then fell, as a percentage of GNP. But food and especially fuel oil fell during the whole postwar era, falling more sharply and with greater fluctuations after 1970.

At the beginning of the postwar period, nondurables made up nearly half of all personal consumption spending, more than services. By 1960 services exceeded nondurables as a share of consumption, and by about 1970 they rose to over half. By 1990 nondurables had fallen to about a third. Some of this may be attributable to the rise of fast-food services, replacing home consumption. But much of the decline stems from the fact that nondurables have a low income-elasticity, meaning the market is easily saturated—once a home is heated adequately, the household will not spend more on heating when its income rises. If markets are to continue to expand, something must rise to compensate for such slower than average growth. That has been services (and to a slight extent, durables). But the growth of services has been slower since 1974 and virtually flat, though volatile, since 1980.

Moreover, from the point of view of generating market demand, the growth of services does less than it might appear to offset the increasing sluggishness in nondurables and the growing volatility of durables, for the largest component in the category of consumer services in the National Income and Product Accounts is the imputed value of the services of owner-occupied housing. These imputed services are not on the market, so the rise of this category does not represent increased spending. When this item is removed, the weakness in the growth of consumer demand after 1970 becomes even more pronounced (see Nell, 1988).

In general, then, the growth of consumption has slowed since the early 1970s, consumption spending has been more volatile, and in composition, spending has shifted markedly away from goods toward services. It has been suggested that this might be viewed as a return to the norm, and that the Golden Age was the exception that needs expla-

Figure 7.3 **FIL of Segmented Trend Through Log of Real Gross Private Domestic Investment — Nonresidential 1947–91**

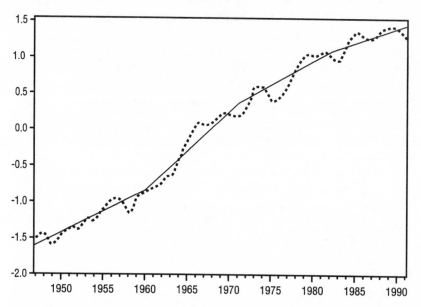

nation. An important feature of the Golden Age was universal military service, which qualified young men for various categories of GI benefits, thereby promoting the formation of stable family consuming units, particularly among the disadvantaged, boosting the demand for durables. With the ending of the draft this disappeared. The War on Poverty might have filled this function—but poverty won that war.

Investment

The pattern evident in consumption spending is repeated in the behavior of investment. This should be no surprise, for investment depends, to a large extent, on the growth of consumption—the slower or more irregularly consumption grows, the lower will the level of investment tend to be, other things being equal (which, of course, they seldom are). First, we can see from a fitting of segmented trends to the log of Real Gross Private Domestic Investment that the growth rate of investment rose in the 1960s, fell back in the 1970s, and then fell again in the 1980s. Moreover, after the late 1960s larger fluctuations are evident.

A look at annual growth rates confirms this. There was one Eisenhower slump in the late 1950s, and the great boom of the mid-1960s; otherwise, the changes in the annual growth rates are relatively small and stay positive or very slightly negative until after 1970. Then there are four large negative growth rates, in 1975, 1983, 1986, and 1990, all more than twice as large as any preceding. There are three substantial positive growth rates, but none as large as in the mid-1960s. Volatility became greater and the overall performance weaker.

This volatility is evident in the cycles of Real Gross Private Domestic Investment. The swings are small up to the mid-60s boom, and up to 1970 the larger swings are positive. After 1970 the swings are much larger, and the largest ones are negative.

Other measures confirm both these developments. For example, using figures drawn from the *IMF Financial Statistics Yearbook*, the ratio of investment to GNP, defined as gross fixed capital formation plus change in stocks, can be seen to have fluctuated much more widely after 1970, and to have trended downward on average. The same trend appears even more sharply in net private domestic nonresidential fixed investment in relation to GNP. There is a sharp drop at the end of the 1940s, a gentle downward drift in the 1950s, with a sharp drop at the end, then a strong rise in the 1960s, followed by much wider fluctuations and a general downward trend through the next two decades.

Just as in consumption, there has been a shift away from manufactured goods, so the composition of investment has shifted from manufacturing to commercial. Business expenditures on new plant and equipment in relation to GNP show a slight rise in the late 1960s, which is maintained, although with larger fluctuations in the second period, but this is made up of a fluctuating and perhaps slightly declining trend in manufacturing plant and equipment combined with a stable and rising trend of expenditures on commercial buildings and equipment.

Some sample figures confirm the impression that investment tended to shift from manufacturing to offices and commercial activities. These figures are from IMF *Staff Papers* (March 1989), and the first two show different categories of expenditure in relation to Gross Fixed Business Investment, the third in relation to total industrial, institutional, and public utility structures (Table 7.4).

Construction

Although private construction is included in private investment, and public construction under government expenditure, the trends in both

Table 7.4

Selected Components of Business Investment

	1958	1986
Computing and accounting machinery	1.3%	16.2%
Electrical and communications equipment	2.8%	9.3%
Commercial structures	9.3%	11.1%

public and private construction are so striking that they deserve special mention.

Taking first net private domestic residential fixed investment in relation to GNP, the trend is strongly downward over the entire period, but the fluctuations become wider after 1970. New housing starts show a somewhat similar picture, although the downward trend is not so noticeable. But the increase in volatility is clear.

Second, the annual growth rates of public construction show a clear downward drift—and increased volatility compared to the 1960s. Recent studies (Aschauer, 1990; Munnell, 1990) have developed a strong case for the claim that public infrastructure spending will promote private productivity growth, and conversely, that the decline in public investment in infrastructure helps to account for the sluggish growth of productivity in the Iron Age. Other studies have come to similar conclusions. A comprehensive survey is presented by Uimonen (1993), together with additional analysis and tests for cointegration and structural stability, which further strengthen the results.

Taking private and public sectors together, construction has been shrinking compared to GNP, and after 1970, came to grow more slowly and turn more volatile. This has meant a loss of high-paying jobs. Public infrastructure has not kept pace with the growth of GNP. OECD figures show a decline in the public capital stock relative to GDP from a peak of 52 percent in the late 1960s to 42 percent in 1990. Gross public investment has similarly turned down (OECD, 1993, p. 75).

Investment depends on the growth of consumption. But on the other hand, consumption depends on investment, since investment creates jobs in the long run and has multiplier effects on income in the short. Thus, the slowdown and increased volatility in each will tend to reinforce those developments in the other. However, these are not the only components of aggregate demand—net exports and government spend-

Figure 7.4 **Net Exports** (billions of 1987$)

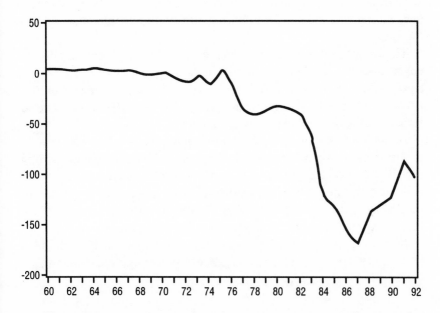

ing will affect incomes and therefore influence consumption; they also could directly influence investment. But we shall see that neither exercised a stabilizing influence.

Net Exports

In principle, foreign trade should be stabilizing. Suppose that at full employment (which should also be full capacity utilization) $X - mY = 0$. Exports, X, will be exogenous; $0 \le m \le 1$ will be the import coefficient. Hence, when aggregate output, Y, rises above the full employment level, the trade balance will turn negative, reducing demand pressure, and when Y falls below full employment, the trade balance will move into surplus, providing a stimulus.

In the Golden Age this almost seemed to be the case. During the first half of the postwar era, net exports provided a small but positive stimulus to the economy. Beginning in the early 1970s, however, this stimulus vanished, reappeared, and then in the mid-1970s disappeared with a vengeance. From then on, net exports were negative, providing a drag on the economy, although they also fluctuated a great deal (see Figure 7.4).

Net exports of consumer durables and nondurables followed very similar patterns. "Other goods" behaved a little differently, recovering very strongly in the early and mid-1980s, before slumping sharply in the late-1980s.

The balance on services, however, developed in a completely different manner. It was slightly negative in the 1960s, turned strongly positive in the 1980s, fell back to zero, and then gained strongly. Investment income also grew strongly in the late 1970s, and after a setback in the mid-1980s, began to recover.

A detailed examination of specific goods shows that the loss of export markets was wide ranging, although computers remained strong until the end of the 1980s. Automobiles turned negative about 1968 and sank steadily thereafter, until turning up somewhat at the end of the 1980s. Industrial supplies went negative briefly in the mid-1970s, but, although fluctuating, remained positive thereafter.

In short, exports went from providing a small but positive stimulus in the early period to creating a large but fluctuating drag on aggregate demand in the second half of the era.

Government

That leaves government as an agent for stabilizing the growth of demand. Suppose at full employment, $G - t = 0$, $T = ty$, where t is the tax rate, and $dG/dy < 0$, $dT/dy > 0$. That is, when aggregate output increases, government spending will diminish, since unemployment insurance and welfare spending will fall, but with higher incomes, tax receipts will rise; and vice versa when Y falls. Overall, therefore, a rise in output will reduce demand stimulus, and a fall will increase it. This requires that the full employment budget be balanced, and that the "automatic stabilizers" be in place. In fact, this has not been the case.

According to the standard propositions of demand management theory, under these circumstances, discretionary policy must be applied. It is the job of fiscal policy to pick up the slack when there is a long-term slowdown, leaving monetary policy, which can be changed more readily, to deal with fluctuations in the short run. So, if long-term developments tend to undermine the ability of effective demand—that is, of markets in the aggregate—to grow sufficiently to maintain the desired level of employment and/or rate of growth of output, taxation and government spending—and other policies—should be adjusted to

Table 7.5

Taxes on Corporate Profits as a Proportion of Government Receipts

1959	18.3%
1965	16.0%
1969	13.5%
1972	11.5%
1979	11.4%
1982	6.5%
1988	9.1%
1991	6.9%

Source: *Economic Report of the President*, 1992, Table B–78.

provide the required stimulus. This is usually thought of as deficit spending—that is, spending in excess of receipts from taxation; but a stimulus is provided even when the budget is balanced, if part or all of the taxation falls on business or household savings.

Taxation and the Deficit

As far as the stabilizing role of a balanced budget is concerned, the composition of taxation, where the burden falls, matters a great deal. In the 1940s and 1950s, taxes on corporate and household savings accounted for almost a quarter of federal revenue. By the 1980s this had fallen to between 5 percent and 10 percent. Table 7.5 shows taxes on corporate profits in relation to total receipts at all levels of government.

So in the 1950s and 1960s the government budget provided a greater stimulus, even without running a deficit. Federal deficits grew substantially in the 1980s, under Reagan and Bush, but this was offset, in part, as all through the postwar era, by state and local surpluses. In 1989, for example, the federal deficit as a proportion of federal revenue, was about 15.5 percent; but the total government deficit was only 6.7 percent of total government revenue. Of this 7.9 percent was raised by taxes on savings. Thus, a balanced budget in the late 1960s, when 15–16 percent of revenue came from corporate taxes, would have provided as much stimulus. Changes in taxation have progressively reduced the impact of government because of the smaller proportion of revenue raised by taxation falling on savings and other withdrawals.

It should be added that the calculation of the deficit leaves much to be desired. Capital items are not treated correctly, and adjustments for inflation and interest rate changes are not made properly (Nell, 1988;

Eisner, 1986). Even if these accounting problems were corrected, however, we would not have in "the deficit" the concept we need, which is a measure of the *stimulus* that the government's budget is providing.

In view of these difficulties, and to get a fuller picture of the way the government has affected the various sectors of the economy, we will examine government spending as a whole, rather than simply assessing the net effect of spending minus taxation.

Government Expenditure

We have seen that all the other major components of aggregate demand came to grow more slowly and to fluctuate more sharply in the second half of the postwar era. Their behavior was also accompanied by a shift away from manufacturing, in both demand and investment, which helped to exacerbate the productivity slowdown, and thus contributed to the virtual collapse of the growth of real wages. What did the government do in response to these changes? Did government spending in fact try to maintain the level and growth of demand? Did it try to move in an offsetting manner, to counteract these disturbing developments?

The straightforward answer, in a nutshell, is that it did nothing of the sort. The expenditures of state and local governments have grown more steadily than those of the federal government. But even state and local spending became more irregular after 1970, slowing down markedly from 1970 to about 1983. Apart from the Korean War and the period 1960–68, total government spending has grown more slowly than GNP. Moreover, perhaps coincidentally, the periods of rapid increase in government spending, late 1940s–early 1950s and 1960–68, were the periods of fastest overall growth and best all-around economic performance (see Figure 7.5).

Breaking down the spending of the federal government, the overall flat level in real terms is made up of more or less offsetting movements in durables and nondurables, combined with spending on services—the largest category—that closely tracks the aggregate pattern, except in the late 1940s–early 1950s. Comparing these movements to GNP growth, it is evident that federal spending has not contributed at all to growth, and, indeed has acted as a drag on growth. In general, government purchasing of both goods and services has declined since the early fifties, though during the decade of the 1960s, government spend-

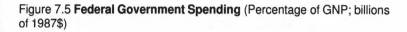

Figure 7.5 **Federal Government Spending** (Percentage of GNP; billions of 1987$)

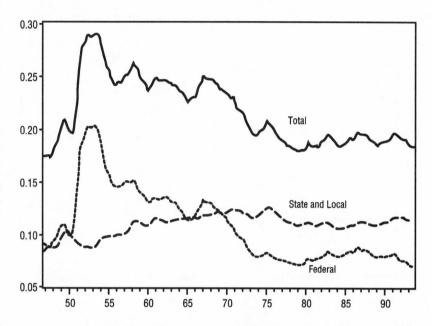

ing remained a stable percentage of GNP. After 1968, however, far from providing an offset to the decline in the growth of private markets, government spending has been shrinking as a percentage of GNP, while staying flat in real terms (see Figure 7.6).

Yet for years there has been an outcry against excessive government spending, and there is a widespread view that "we don't have the money" to increase government spending. Part of this can be explained by the fact that some controversial elements in the government budget *have* been growing faster than GNP. This can be seen by comparing government expenditure on structures and expenditure on net interest payments and transfer payments.

Government spending on structures contributes to the demand for construction and manufacturing and therefore provides a strong stimulus. It also helps the growth of productivity by providing public infrastructure. By contrast, expenditure on transfers and net interest provides much less stimulus and contributes little or nothing to productivity. Spending on structures grew rapidly in the late 1940s–early 1950s, declined in the Eisenhower years, showed a little strength in the

Figure 7.6 **Federal Government Purchases, Nonmilitary: Durables, Nondurables, Services** (billions of 1987$)

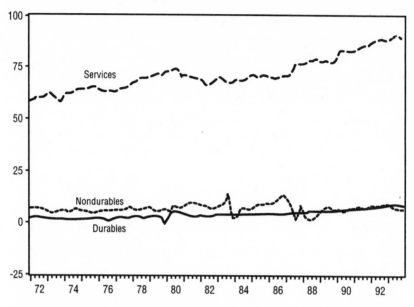

1960s, and declined precipitously until 1980, after which it rose slightly. The fact that it has diminished as a percent of GNP contributes to the slowing of market growth. Transfer payments, however, grew strongly during the whole postwar period, at a substantially faster rate than GNP. Some transfer payments, such as unemployment insurance, contribute to maintaining demand and behave countercyclically. Welfare payments, pensions and Social Security, and medical payments meet important social needs, and at the same time enable their recipients to purchase goods and services. So they contribute to the maintenance and/or development of demand, but they probably contribute more to the demand for services than to the demand for goods. Finally, net interest payments began to rise in the 1960s, and have risen very steeply since 1970, much faster than GNP. But net interest payments contribute little or nothing to the development of demand (see Figure 7.7).

Much of the outcry over government spending has been generated by the rapid growth of transfer payments and the rising cost of the federal debt. Both have risen at an exceptional rate and concern over both is understandable. But the overall government market for goods

Figure 7.7 **Components of Government Spending as a Percent of GNP**
(billions of 1987$)

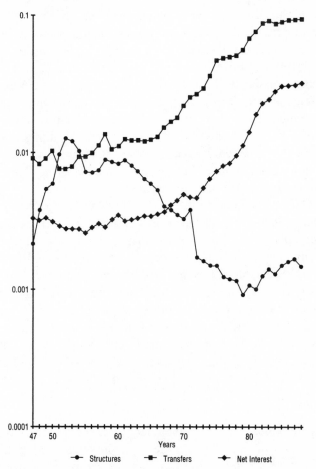

and services has failed to grow in real terms and therefore has actually declined in relation to GNP, creating an important drag on growth rather than providing the stimulus that was needed.

Lessons

What does this survey teach us? First, the resources for faster growth, higher levels of output and income are available. The poor economic performance of the second half of the postwar era is not due to lack of resources, but to the fact that the labor and productive capacity already in place have not been put to use.

It also suggests that poor performance is cumulative or self-reinforcing in a number of new ways not present in the economy in the earlier period. As demand grows more slowly, and becomes more volatile, while shifting toward services, investment also slows down, becomes more volatile, and shifts away from plant and equipment toward commercial activities and offices. It is not implausible to read this as interacting cause and effect: aggregate demand slows down and becomes more volatile, so investment follows suit. Multiplier theory would suggest that this could have the result that aggregate demand might slow down even more, or become even more volatile. The interaction would exacerbate the initial effect.

The same kind of cumulative interaction might come about another, more important, way. Consider the impact of the slowdown in demand growth on productivity. With weaker demand, and a shift in the composition of investment, productivity growth can be expected to slow down. But this means that real wages will now grow more slowly, and disparities between wages and salaries are likely to widen. This in turn will create consumer uncertainty, and lead to slower growth in household spending, that is, it will exacerbate the trends in consumption. But this in turn will react back on investment, through the capital stock adjustment principle, reducing the growth of capacity. This will further reduce productivity growth, in a deepening spiral. In short, an unstable cumulative interaction could develop between demand and productivity growth.

This may help also to explain the changes in the unemployment-inflation tradeoff. In the Golden Age unemployment and inflation moved inversely, while in the Iron Age they appear to have moved together. Or at any rate, the tradeoff, if it could still be identified, shifted out several times. Had this not happened, governments might have been much less inclined to adopt austerity, knowing that if inflation developed they could easily control it. But if the three changes in the pattern of demand growth brought a slowdown in productivity growth, the effect could well have been to raise unit labor costs. This could happen if productivity growth became more *uneven* while wage settlements were obliged to maintain traditional relativities. Sectors in which productivity was rising would make settlements based on productivity gains, but other sectors would insist on maintaining their traditional relationship. This would lead to pressure for price increases, and at the same time could undermine U.S. competitiveness, leading to rising imports and a weaker exchange rate. (OECD data show that U.S. unit labor costs in the 1980s rose faster than those of U.S. trading partners; OECD, 1993, p. 64.) Thus, a slowdown in growth, accompanied by a rise in volatility and a shift away from manufacturing, could have led to inflationary pressures through the effects on productivity and thus on unit labor costs. The point can only be suggested here, but it may be an important part of the story.

Other factors also led inflation and unemployment to move together. Inflation has many causes. First, the oil shock increased a basic price, one that entered directly or indirectly into the costs of almost everything. This set off a cost inflation spiral. But at the same time the oil shock caused a deterioration of the balance of trade, which reduced aggregate demand and therefore tended to raise unemployment. Hence, the two moved together. Second, attempts to control inflation through severe monetary restrictions raise interest rates and make them more volatile. When the restrictions are severe enough, they cause unemployment to increase; but the additional uncertainty over credit and the higher charges for interest add to the costs of business. This tends to lead to increased markups, at least in those sectors where businesses have a degree of control over prices—empirically, most of the economy. Thus, monetarist policies can, in certain circumstances, lead to price increases while unemployment is rising.

The slowdown in the growth of markets, especially in the second half of the era, was quite widespread. It shows up in all components of aggregate demand, as does the increase in volatility and the shift away from manufactured products toward services. This is not likely to be the consequence of policy; rather, it is part of the pattern of development and capital accumulation. The emergence of new technologies has created uncertainty among investing firms over whether and when to invest in a new process or product—and whether and when to abandon an old. The new forms of communication have permitted long-distance detailed control over production processes, making it possible to locate plants in distant, and low-wage, regions, and at the same time have made it easier to shift capital funds about. One result has been the emergence of worldwide competition, together with worldwide sourcing. This has led, in turn, to growth in world trade.

But a rise in world trade can have a perverse effect. Nations are not equally competitive; a rise in trade benefits nations unequally, leading to balance of payments deficits for some and surpluses for others. Deficit nations thus tend to contract, surplus ones to expand; and this is supposed to lead to adjustment. But surplus countries cannot expand above full employment. Nor will they be willing to permit their exchange rate to rise without limit. Deficit nations, likewise, will not be willing to permit a free fall in their currency. Moreover, if imports are inelastic, devaluation triggers inflation. Hence, contraction of income in the deficit countries has become the chief means of adjustment. A rise in trade, therefore, can lead to a rise in unemployment. Far from providing a stimulus, more trade can lead to stagnation.

Rather than offsetting these changes, the policy measures actually pursued in the 1970s and 1980s made things worse. Instead of enlarging government purchases, especially of goods, taking measures to support investment at home so as to diminish its volatility, and taking action to improve the balance of payments, successive administrations cut back on government, deregulated and even encouraged capital flight, and threw open our markets, allowing our foreign balance to deteriorate. This is not to deny that a case could be made for these policies, or some of them at least, on long-term grounds. But such gains, if any, must be balanced against the costs of the stagnation that they bring in their wake.

Policy Implications

The preceding suggests that policy should be devoted to offsetting the pattern of growth slowdown and volatility increase. The problem, then, is not that government has become too large and is growing too fast, as is commonly believed, but that it is too small and has been growing too slowly. Government spending underwent the same changes that we found in private spending—it stagnated, increased in volatility, and shifted away from manufacturing toward services. In particular, there has been too little devoted to public investment in infrastructure, education, health, transportation, R&D, protection of the environment, and related areas—all areas in which well-managed government spending, which would contribute to the growth of demand, would also help to promote productivity growth.

Why did government fail? This is a complex matter. One reason is that the Democratic party in the second period favored austerity.

Worldwide, the advanced countries all faced difficulties in the second period. But a few succeeded with expansionist governments. Austria, Japan, Norway, and Sweden, for example, managed to maintain growth with high employment and low inflation, as did Germany until the austerity-minded Kohl government came to power.

But the new relationships also make it clear that old-fashioned expansion through fiscal and monetary policies won't do the job. Even a wisely managed expansion of government activity, increasing demand and promoting productivity, could get into trouble. For a policy sufficient to offset the changes that have led to the U.S. economy's poor performance would require establishing a strong and persistent stimulus to demand, one that will grow faster than GNP now is growing. But the evidence suggests that this could lead to a substantial rise in imports, leading to pressure against the dollar, perhaps setting off speculation and a run on the dollar. Even with no growth, a lower exchange rate, accompanied by a sharp rise in demand, could lead to increases in the prices of primary products, so that a round of inflation might be triggered. In the present political climate this is not acceptable, in spite of the fact that the real costs of lost output due to unemployment are generally estimated to be far greater than any real costs associated with inflation. Moreover, if price inflation outruns wage inflation, real wages will fall, cutting back consumption, and this may have a negative effect on investment. Expansion is no longer a simple matter.

However, if a U.S. expansion were accompanied by expansionist policies on the part of our major trading partners, then our exports would rise as well. Imports might rise still faster, but the pressure against the dollar would be much less, and consequently there would be less likelihood of inflation. This would have to be a systematic, coordinated expansion, jointly managed by all major advanced countries, with arrangements for financing any trade deficits caused by the expansion. Buffer stocks could be developed, under international auspices, to prevent unacceptable primary price increases when demand rises. In other words, the barriers to an expansionary policy can be overcome by redesigning policy in ways that have been proposed before, notably by Nicholas Kaldor. However, such an approach requires a degree of international cooperation that is not imaginable at present. It also requires a commitment to develop coordinated expansion policies. Unfortunately, there are only limited institutional arrangements for international cooperation, and the political climate favors austerity.

Helpful though it would be, if difficult to arrange, even coordinated international expansion would not be enough. For it is not just expansion that is required; it is long-term management of the transition to a new technological framework. Keynesian policies were essentially short term. To manage long-term development requires experienced managers, trained in policy issues, and equipped with the necessary powers. It must be possible to impose short-term price controls, for example, if inflation tends to get out of hand, or to halt trading if speculation threatens a run on the dollar.

But short-term measures are of little use unless they are based on well-thought-out long-term policies. In the long run, preventing inflation will require a domestic incomes policy, either a tax-based incomes policy (TIP) or a "social contract"—carefully worked out. To maintain a strong dollar, there must be a reasonable balance on foreign accounts, which requires investment and technology policies to encourage a strong competitive position. In addition, there must be cooperation among central banks to prevent speculative runs.

The message of the policy failures in the last twenty years is that long-term demand management must also include encouraging productivity growth and the development of competitive positions in new technologies. Incomes policies may help to prevent wage inflation, but even with inflation under control and employment high, in the long run things could turn sour if investment is inadequate or wrongly directed. So there will have to be investment policies to encourage the right amount and type of capital expansion, and, as well, to control its volatility, on the other. So investment and incomes policies will have to be developed together, to prevent the kind of cumulative interaction we found between the slowdown in demand and the slowdown in productivity growth. (Investment policy deserves a separate discussion, but government assumption of risk in the introduction of new technology dates back to World War II.)

Why not leave it all to the free market? The theory of transformational growth tells us that is not a possible answer. The "free market," that is, a self-adjusting market working through flexible prices, flourished in the last century and gradually gave way to the multiplier-accelerator system of mass production, which may now be yielding to new patterns of adjustment. Traces of flex-price markets can still be found in the advanced countries and are widespread in the craft-based sectors of the developing world. Otherwise free markets, with deficits crowding out productive investment and savings governing growth, exist only in the imaginations of conservative economists. In fact, private consumption, private investment, and the trade balance have all slowed down. To fall back on "nonintervention" is to accept long-term stagnation. It also endangers our competitive position. The new technologies are so expensive and so risky that without government participation, licensing, and regulation, companies will not be able to undertake the investment. Moreover, without regulation, the public will be endangered—think of the implications of a mistake in genetic engineering.

In short, for a return to prosperity, new international policies are needed, and a new spirit of cooperation directed toward promoting joint expansion. These must be complemented by new long-term domestic policies. It is a tall order. But as Mrs. Thatcher said in a different context: "There is no alternative."

8

Full Employment and the Inflation Constraint

Thomas I. Palley

Introduction

Twenty-five years ago, if you asked a representative economist what constituted full employment, the reply would likely have been that it corresponded to a situation with 4 percent unemployment. (The figure of 4 percent was the full-employment benchmark used in the study on the inflation-unemployment problem contained in *Studies by the Staff of the Cabinet Committee on Price Stability*, published by the U.S. Government Printing Office in 1969.) A more optimistic economist might even have suggested 3 percent unemployment. Another viable candidate for the definition of full employment might have been that proposed by Sir William Beveridge in his *Full Employment in a Free Society* (1944, p. 18) as a situation in which the number of job vacancies is greater than or equal to the number of unemployed workers. This is not fanciful speculation, but rather reflects thinking that was then current in the economics profession. Indeed, these very definitions were considered in James Tobin's 1971 presidential address to the American Economic Association.

If there was some uncertainty over the precise definition of full employment, it is also likely that most professional economists would have regarded unemployment rates in excess of 5 percent as warranting stimulative monetary and fiscal interventions. Today (December 1993) the official U.S. unemployment rate is 6.4 percent. Moreover, on the basis of recent releases from the Bureau of Labor Statistics' revealing response biases in the household unemployment survey, this number is probably understated by a half percentage point.

Table 8.1

Average Rates of Unemployment in the United States

1950.1–1959.4	4.5%
1960.1–1969.4	4.8%
1970.1–1979.4	6.2%
1980.1–1991.2	7.1%

Source: Citibase.

It is also clear that this higher rate of unemployment is not just a temporary result of the recent recession; rather, it reflects a trend established over two decades. Table 8.1 shows the quarterly average unemployment rates for the U.S. economy by decade, and its message is clear. For the decade 1950.1–1959.4, the average rate of unemployment was 4.5 percent; for the decade 1960.1–1969.4, the average rate was 4.8 percent; for the decade 1970.1–1979.4, it was 6.2 percent; and finally, for the period 1980.1–1991.2, it was 7.1 percent.

Though there are expressions of concern with the current magnitude of unemployment, for the most part both politicians and the public fatalistically accept it as something that they are able to do little about. This fatalism is bolstered by the economics profession, which now counsels against activist policy. Arguments for expansionary fiscal policy are rebuffed on the grounds that the federal deficit is already enormous. Arguments for expansionary monetary policy are rebuffed on the grounds that it would only cause inflation, and would have no sustained impact on output and employment.

These views have transformed the intellectual landscape governing the construction of economic policy. Rebutting the claim that activist monetary policy produces only accelerating inflation has therefore become an essential prerequisite for creating the conditions under which policies geared to full employment can again be adopted. If unaccomplished, advocates of such policies must face being written off on the grounds that their policies are not viable because of "economic realities." The consequence will be a tragic continuation of the recent history of unemployment.

Economists and the Retreat from Full Employment

In making the case for a return of high employment policies, let me begin with a critical review of the role played by the economics profession in bringing about the retreat from full employment. To many people, academic economists engage in creating abstractions that bear little relevance for the "real" world. This position is epitomized in the expression (so galling for economists) "If you're so clever, how come you're not rich?" Though the ideas of economists may not influence the conscious behavior of people, their influence can still be very powerful and may be felt in unconscious ways. In a famous passage concluding *The General Theory*, Keynes wrote of this influence:

> The ideas of economists and political philosophers, both when they are right and when they are wrong, are more powerful than is commonly understood. Indeed the world is ruled by little else. Practical men, who believe themselves to be quite exempt from intellectual influences, are usually the slaves of some defunct economist. Madmen in authority, who hear voices in the air, are distilling their frenzy from the academic scribblers of a few years back. (p. 383)

The message that Keynes sought to convey is that academic economists create economic knowledge, and that this knowledge, albeit in popularized forms, becomes the lens through which people view the economy. Since this lens substantially determines what we see, it also therefore determines what we perceive as our needs, and what we perceive as possible. Nowhere is this pattern more true than in the history of the inflation constraint and the debate about the effects of monetary policy.

The 1960s marked the high-water point of Keynesian economic policy. During that decade there was a widespread belief that monetary and fiscal policy could be successfully used to permanently achieve full employment. However, even then economists were aware that higher rates of employment automatically involved accepting a higher rate of inflation. This was the inescapable tradeoff made famous by the Phillips curve.

Beginning in the late 1960s and continuing through the 1970s, U.S. inflation began to worsen. This worsening was brought about by a number of events, including excessive demand pressure resulting from the Vietnam War mobilization, social conflict that spilled over into conflict over income distribution, a world commodity price boom in 1972 brought about by a global economic boom, a decline in the trend rate of U.S. productivity growth, and three successive oil price shocks in 1973, 1976, and 1979. However, rather than supplementing Phillips curve theory with a multicausal theory of inflation, the economics profession rejected the Phillips curve in favor of a monocausal theory at the core of which stands the concept of the natural rate of unemployment.

The argument behind this theory is that if unemployment falls below the natural rate, inflation will increase; moreover, inflation will accelerate as long as unemployment remains below the natural rate. In later versions of natural rate theory that include rational expectations, there is no tradeoff at all. Systematic monetary policy can't lower the rate of unemployment, and any attempts to do so just produce higher inflation (Lucas, 1973). Since accelerating and ever higher rates of inflation are unacceptable, the policy message from natural rate theory is clear: the unemployment rate should not be allowed to fall below the natural rate of unemployment. Consequently, macroeconomic policy is rigidly bound by an inflation constraint.

The intellectual arguments for the natural rate hypothesis have been bolstered by its rhetorical adoption of the "natural" metaphor, which implies that anything other than the natural rate is "unnatural." If the natural rate were identified with rates of 1 or 2 percent unemployment, adoption of the theory would be of little significance. However, once the natural rate is defined as 6–7 percent unemployment, its adoption implies that the economy must operate with much higher levels of unemployment. The result is huge and unnecessary social and economic costs.

Worse than that, by adopting the language of free markets and perfectly competitive equilibrium, natural rate theory subtly entraps policy makers into the belief that the *actual* rate is the *natural* rate. Thus, as macroeconomic performance has faltered over the last two decades, this has led to the notion of a rising natural rate. In the face of persistently rising unemployment, policy makers have been enjoined to do nothing, since actual unemployment represents the natural working of the free market, and trying to reduce unemployment would only contribute to higher inflation.

Introduced by Edmund Phelps (1967) and Milton Friedman (1968), the theory of the natural rate was initially confined to laissez-faire academic economists and conservative think tanks. But in the past twenty years it has spread into the highest counsels of economic policy making. This is captured in the *Economic Report of the President*, a document that is drafted each year by the president's Council of Economic Advisers.

Table 8.2

The Changing Measure of Full Employment in the
Economic Report of the President

1970	3.8%
1979	5.1%
1983	6–7.0%

Source: D. M. Gordon, 1987.

Table 8.2 shows the changing measure of full employment as reported in the *Economic Report*. In 1970, the report declared 3.8 percent unemployment as the definition of full employment and used that as the basis for computing the economy's maximum "potential output." In the 1979 *Economic Report* the official definition of full employment was revised to 5.1 percent (1979, pp. 72–74). By 1983, the triumph of natural rate theory was so complete, that the new term "inflation threshold unemployment rate" (1983, p. 37) was introduced, thereby escaping from the responsibility of ensuring full employment. Moreover, this new inflation threshold unemployment rate was declared to "probably lie between 6 and 7 percent" (1983, p. 37).

How Binding Is the Inflation Constraint?

Behind the natural rate theory of unemployment lies the vision of a binding inflation constraint that handcuffs monetary policy. Yet this vision is a contestable vision. An alternative vision is one in which the economy is in permanent disequilibrium owing to persistent shocks to different sectors, and monetary policy can help reduce the resulting unemployment.

This alternative vision can be understood through the following metaphor. Adjustment in real world economies is akin to an "escalator" process, through which markets adjust back to equilibrium slowly. In such economies this escalator adjustment process can be speeded up by interventions on the part of the monetary authority that controls the rate of nominal demand growth. By contrast, natural rate economies (Lucas, 1973) are "elevator" economies, in which adjustment is instantaneous: consequently, there is no role for monetary policy in facilitating the adjustment process, and to the extent that policy-sponsored nominal demand growth is uncertain, it may actually disrupt the economy by sending the elevator to the wrong floor.

To understand how this metaphor operates, consider a person trying to get to the top of an escalator. If the escalator is stationary, the time taken to reach the top depends on the level of climbing effort. Now suppose the escalator is set in motion. In this case, the time to the top is reduced by the underlying movement of the escalator, but this reduction may in part be offset by reduced climbing effort. As long as the reduction in climbing effort is not too drastic, then time taken to reach the top is reduced by increasing the speed of the escalator.

This escalator metaphor is instructive for understanding the Keynesian view of how markets adjust, with the speed of the escalator acting as a proxy for the speed of adjustment of prices and wages. In all markets, price adjustment is slow, owing to problems of uncertainty and incomplete information. This problem of slow adjustment is particularly acute in labor markets because of the inevitable conflict of interest between firms and workers over the distribution of income, which in turn leads workers to be wary of opportunistic behavior by firms.

When this microeconomic description of the process of market adjustment is placed within a multisector economy, in which individual sectors are subject to random demand shocks, unemployment inevitably emerges. (This description of the microeconomic foundations of the inflation-unemployment tradeoff was first presented by Tobin, 1972. A formal model of such an economy is provided by Palley, 1994.)

In sectors with unemployment, relative prices are too high given the level of sectoral demand. Restoration of full employment therefore calls for relative price reductions, but this process is slow and contested. Instead, the monetary authority can cause nominal demand to grow, and this mitigates the need for price adjustment in depressed sectors. Monetary policy can therefore be used to speed up the adjustment process and acts in a fashion analogous to speeding up the escalator. However, it also causes inflation in sectors at full employment.

The increase in inflation then produces a response by labor market participants. To the extent that they respond by incorporating inflation expectations into the nominal wage adjustment process, the employment effects of nominal demand growth are reduced. If agents fully incorporate inflation expectations, nominal demand growth is fully neutralized by increases in wages and costs.

According to the above description, increasing the rate of nominal demand growth acts akin to speeding up the adjustment escalator, and this reduces the duration of disequilibrium and the extent of unemployment. The incorporation of inflation expectations into nominal wages is analogous to reducing climbing effort in response to speeding up of the escalator. If there is full incorporation of inflation expectations even in sectors with significant unemployment, then the only effect of stimulative monetary policy will be higher inflation. This is because all the effect of demand growth will be directed into higher wages and prices. It is this very special assumption that underlies natural rate theory.

Elsewhere (Palley, 1993b) I have formally modeled the above and have estimated the model. Let me now report some of these findings and suggest their policy implications. The model involves estimating a relationship between inflation and the duration of spells of unemployment. This is then combined with a relation between total unemployment and unemployment duration, to provide a relation between inflation and unemployment. This relation is what used to be called a Phillips curve, and it provides an indication of the tradeoff between inflation and unemployment.

The equilibrium rate of unemployment is determined as follows

$$U = [Q/L] \times D \qquad (1)$$

where U = unemployment rate, Q = number of separations from employment each week, L = labor force, D = average duration (weeks) of a spell of unemployment.

The equation estimating the average duration of unemployment spells for the U.S. economy was

$$D = 1.07 + 0.64D (-1) + 0.67U (-1) - 0.08EINF - 0.04UINF \qquad (2)$$
$$(3.32) (16.72) \qquad (0.36) \qquad (-4.45) \qquad (-1.48)$$

$$\text{Adj.}R^2 = 0.98, \text{ D.W.} = 2.03, \qquad AR(1) = 0.44$$
$$(4.80)$$

$EINF$ = expected inflation, $UINF$ = unexpected inflation. The sample period was 1961.3–1991.3. Figures in parentheses are t-statistics. The values for $EINF$ and $UINF$ were obtained from an ordinary least squares equation estimating inflation. In accordance with the methodology for constructing estimates of expected inflation popularized by Barro (1976, 1977), *UINF* was identified with the residuals from this equation, while *EINF* was identified with the fitted values of the equation. The inflation equation is reported in Palley (1993).

Unfortunately, data on separations are not available. The normal value of *Q/L* was therefore proxied by the "average" value of *U/D* = 0.45 computed over the equation sample period. Combining equations (1) and (2), and using the proxied value for separations per worker of 0.45, yields a putative inflation-unemployment tradeoff given by

$$U = 7.89 - 0.75EINF - 0.41UINF \qquad (3)$$

In this estimate, the tradeoff coefficient is −0.75: that is, every 1 percent point increase in the equilibrium rate of inflation reduces unemployment by 0.75 percent points. The putative tradeoff provided by the model yields the following inflation-unemployment combinations:

3 percent inflation–5.64 percent unemployment
5 percent inflation–4.14 percent unemployment
7 percent inflation–2.64 percent unemployment

These results suggest a definitive and not unfavorable tradeoff between inflation and unemployment. They can then be combined with Okun's law to provide estimates of the output-inflation tradeoff; this gives us a measure of the output lost for each point that the inflation rate is reduced. This derivation may be expressed schematically as:

1 percent increase INFLATION

(Phillips tradeoff = −0.75)

→ 0.75 percent decrease UNEMPLOYMENT

(Okun tradeoff = −2.50)

→ 1.875 percent increase OUTPUT = $112.5 billion

Conventional estimates of Okun's law place the Okun coefficient at −2.5: that is, a 1 percent decline in the rate of unemployment increases the level of output by 2.5 percentage points. Combining Okun's law with the above estimates of the Phillips tradeoff produces an output-inflation tradeoff of 1.875; that is, a 1 percent increase in inflation produces a 1.875 percent increase in the level of output. Given current dollar GNP of $6 trillion, this implies that a 1 percent increase in the rate of inflation would increase GNP by $112.5 billion. In per capita terms, given a population of 255 million, an increase of 1 percent in the inflation rate would provide additional income of $441 for every man, woman, and child in the United States. This clearly reveals the significant costs of pursuing a low-inflation policy.

Conclusion

The above analysis does not answer what inflation and employment policy should be. Instead, it seeks to dispel the notion of a binding inflation constraint as promulgated by natural rate theory. Over the last fifteen years, the American public has been sold a false bill of goods and told that it has no choice when it comes to the inflation constraint. The inflation constraint has therefore been used to silence debate and prejudice the issue in favor of a low inflation policy favorable to financial interests. It is therefore time to reassess this policy commitment and honestly confront the huge costs (in the form of unemployment and lost output) that it entails.

Reopening the debate is a first step. A second step involves constructing a viable policy configuration that can lower unemployment. Over the last two decades the U.S. economy has experienced a progressive weakening of private-sector aggregate demand. In the late 1980s this was obscured by the explosion in household and corporate debt levels, but it has been starkly revealed by the recent demand-led recession, which occurred despite (1) the enormous federal budget deficit, and (2) the low rate of household saving. In the 1960s, given these conditions, such a demand-induced recession would have been inconceivable. Instead, the huge deficit and low saving rates would have been strongly inflationary.

Restoring the vitality of private-sector aggregate demand is the prerequisite for a sustained reduction in unemployment. This will undoubtedly require accommodating monetary policy. However, fiscal policy must also play a significant role, and it is here that the current budget deficit enters as a novel and problematic constraint. Given that expansionary increases in expenditures or generalized reductions in taxes are not possible, the role of fiscal policy must be forcefully redirected toward the link between income distribution and aggregate demand. Though the level of government expenditures and taxes may be shackled by the government's budget constraint, their composition is free to vary so as to achieve improved distributional outcomes. In this fashion, the weight of fiscal policy can be shifted to counter the economy's internally adverse distributional forces, which have been an important cause of the weakening in private-sector aggregate demand.

Possible changes in the composition of taxation and tax expenditures include (1) a shift toward the taxation of income derived from dividends and interest and away from taxation on earned income derived from wages; (2) increased progressivity of income taxes; (3) reducing the ceiling on tax-deductible mortgages—after all, tax-deductible mortgage interest was designed to encourage a home-owning democracy, not to provide subsidies to ownership of palatial homes; (4) elimination of the federal deduction from state income, property, and real estate taxes; (5) imposition of reasonable ceilings on amounts that corporations can give in the form of tax-free pension benefits—a loophole that has subsidized substantial tax-free savings for the higher-paid echelons of society.

9

Stimulating Global Employment Growth

Lance Taylor

For the two or three centuries that capitalism has dominated the world system, deep-rooted socioeconomic forces overlain by economic and political cycles have determined the level and growth of productive employment; in the Braudelian *longue durée* "full employment" has not been the normal state of affairs. Since the 1970s, in particular, structure and conjuncture have limited job creation and per capita income growth. Policies are on hand to counteract these failures. For them to be fully effective, however, profound institutional changes will have to occur.

Economic factors influencing employment are analyzed here, mainly with diagrams to illustrate the implications of theoretical models applicable to both developed and developing economies. The main conclusions go as follows:

(1) Trends in labor productivity and demand composition at the sectoral level have to be in balance for full employment to be attained. In traditional language, problems of both realization and disproportionality can arise and must be dealt with directly. High rates of employment in connection with ongoing productivity growth may ultimately require reduced labor force participation rates or a shorter normal period of work, even with healthy expansion of aggregate demand.

(2) The way in which economic activity responds to changes in the income distribution can also be problematical. Reductions in unit labor costs from greater productivity are most easily absorbed if

aggregate demand increases with higher profits. If the economy is not profit-led in this sense, Luddite arguments for employment support by restraint of productivity gains (with deleterious effects on long-run growth) are valid. In many developing economies, demand appears to be stimulated by a rising share of wages, not profits, making proactive policy necessary to generate the exports and investment needed to absorb higher productivity.

(3) Historical experience in developing countries also suggests that market intervention rather than laissez-faire price signals may be required to kick off productivity growth in the first place. This observation runs directly counter to the "hands off" industrial policy stance now recommended by agencies such as the World Bank.

(4) In the short to medium run, employment growth in developing economies can easily be supply-constrained, especially by scarce foreign exchange. Policy packages to overcome this barrier are complex and involve a substantial degree of market intervention.

(5) Paradoxically, an ample supply of foreign exchange is also not easy to use. In an inappropriate policy environment, it may not feed into higher investment and can spill over into capital flight.

(6) In industrialized economies where demand tends to be profit-led, policies aimed at expanding employment can be frustrated by internal distributional conflicts. Feedbacks of wage pressure into labor militancy, flagging investment demand, and balance of payments pressures can frustrate expansionary policy. Institutional changes in the labor market, taxes or controls on capital movements, expanded public investment programs, and other market-modifying interventions can help raise employment growth. However, the current political climate with its emphasis on financial rectitude does not favor such actions. Political elites in the industrialized economies have convinced themselves that elections are lost because of inflation, not stagnant wages or absent jobs. Such attitudes may now be shifting, but no one can foresee how rapidly or to what extent the conventional wisdom will reverse.

The Long Run

Economic theory does not handle the long-run factors affecting employment growth very well; a "steady state" or "center of gravitation" in a formal model is bound to be a poor approximation to the configuration toward which the economic system is actually tending. The results with most credibility follow from accounting balances consistent with steady growth. They can be illustrated with a series of diagrams tying together per capita consumption, labor expended per unit output, unit labor costs, and the level of employment in various combinations. We begin by looking at the macroeconomic consistency conditions that must be satisfied if full employment is to be attained.

Realization and Disproportionality

Suppose that the economy is growing, with some sectors expanding more rapidly than others. Also assume that there are ongoing labor productivity increases across sectors, with their labor/output ratios declining at different rates. Can such trends go together with full employment?

In general the answer is no. One can see why in a few steps. Figure 9.1 illustrates the situation at the macro level with all sectors summed to an aggregate-like gross domestic product (or GDP). Demand for output per person (total demand D divided by population P) is d, and the labor-output ratio is $l = \pi \, \sigma. (P/Q)$, where π is the labor force participation rate (the share of the population that works), σ is the share of a person's time devoted to work ("the length of the working day"), and Q is output. If there is to be full employment, the condition:

$$ld = 1 \qquad (1)$$

must apply. In other words, labor per unit output and demand per unit labor must be in balance if demand is to support a full-employment output level (Pasinetti, 1981; Taylor, 1994a).

This relationship presents two difficulties over time. The first is that l decreases when there is labor productivity growth, which historically runs between zero and a few percent per year under modern capitalism. Second, although per capita demand for a given commodity or service may rise for a time, ultimately it tends to slow or even decline. For example, in the United States in the 1920s and Europe after World War II, surging consumption of automobiles and associated products supported employment growth, even though productivity was going up. By now in these economies, cars are not income-elastic items and their demand growth will be limited by population expansion and scrapping rates, despite the best efforts of the advertising industry.

Meanwhile, productivity increases implicit in automation and just-in-time inventory scheduling will lead to negative employment growth in the motor vehicle sector.

Figure 9.1 illustrates these problems. The full-employment condition $ld = 1$ is represented by the solid curve (a rectangular hyperbola). The two arrows show that both the labor/output ratio l and demand d tend to fall from initial values consistent with full employment. In an economy with many (say, N) products, this balance relationship generalizes in obvious fashion to

$$l_1 d_1 + l_2 d_2 + \ldots + l_N d_N = 1 \qquad (2)$$

where the subscripts label the l and d ratios in each sector i.

Strictly speaking, in a situation of stable growth, the l_i coefficients should stand for direct-and-indirect (through input-output and capital coefficient matrixes) labor inputs required to support public and private consumption and net exports by sector; the d_i coefficients should sum up these different sources of demand per capita (see Taylor, 1994a).

There are bound to be complicated trends in the variables in this equation. As noted above, the l_i coefficients will generally be falling, while some d_i may be rising, as demand surges for new products, while others will be going down as consumer saturation sets in. If both d_i and l_i are decreasing in sector i, then it will lose jobs in absolute numbers. A rising d_j may offset a falling l_j in another sector j, generating employment growth. Obvious examples are service sectors in the United States in the 1980s, which had rising demands and very slow rates of productivity growth, which combined to create many jobs—a few with high remunerations and the big majority with close to minimum wages.

These observations suggest that one of capitalism's major devices for supporting ongoing employment growth has been the continual introduction of new commodities and services and the elimination of old ones—in the familiar example, when cars entered the popular consumption basket, the buggy whip industry fell on hard times. Such processes are bound to be episodic and difficult to predict. There is no automatic mechanism that makes the $l_i d_i$ terms for currently functioning sectors in (2) add up to one.

Figure 9.1 **Effects of Productivity Growth and Demand Saturation on Overall Employment**

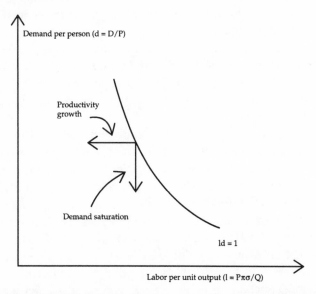

Note: The rectangular hyperbola $ld = 1$ defines full employment. Saturation of consumption reduces demand per person d, while productivity growth reduces labor required per unit output, 1. Offsetting factors could include reductions in the labor force participation rate, π, or the average share of time spent working ("the length of the working day"), σ.

In hoary language, (2) can fail to be satisfied due to either a realization or a disproportionality problem. Figure 9.1 shows how demand saturation and productivity growth may go together to hold down availability of work—full employment may simply not be realized. Even if enough work is available in principle, disproportional demand and productivity trends across sectors may require substantial labor force reallocations if full employment is to be maintained. Such movements are never socially simple; most countries rely on public action to make them as painless as possible.

If the employment realization—or stagnation—problem is severe, it can be offset in several ways, but all entail their own complications. One possibility, discussed more fully below, is an attempt at demand stimulation by a real wage increase or progressive income redistribution more generally.

Others are reductions in the participation rate, π, and/or the share of time devoted to work, σ. However, such tendencies can be offset by other social forces. In most industrialized economies, female participation rates have risen steadily in the face of stagnant income levels. This adjustment has permitted households to buy all the new goods (including public consumption items "purchased" via taxes) that have entered the market over the past twenty or thirty years. How many families had personal computers or big-screen TVs combined with VCRs in 1975? How many have more than one member working in the 1990s so that they can afford these new "necessities"?

Despite recently increasing participation and unshortened work efforts, it is certainly conceivable that the process of throwing new goods on the market in rich economies may slacken off, especially if environmental constraints begin to bite. In such a case, condition (2) will become increasingly difficult to satisfy—the length of the working day (or week) will have to fall if current participation rates are to be maintained. This logic underlies proposals such as those of Schor (1991) that working time should be reduced in the industrial economies. Some recent western European political events point in this direction.

As the models about to be developed suggest, the hitch with such schemes is that in the absence of productivity growth, simply sharing the labor hours required for a given level of output among more people would reduce average payments to those previously employed—not necessarily a politically acceptable move. Even worse, under adverse circumstances higher productivity can lead to reduced labor demand overall. There is no future guarantee that introducing new objects of demand or adjusting the length of the working day will overcome the realization problems inherent in the market system.

Labor Payments and Costs

The classic mechanism enabling real per capita demand to rise under capitalism has been growth of real wages in line with productivity increases—in terms of Figure 9.1, the real wage w increases to offset reductions in labor inputs l by supporting a growing aggregate per capita demand level d. However, this process can break down. Even if wages do go up to offset lower labor/output ratios, productivity growth does not necessarily lead to higher output and employment.

This possibility dawned on the Luddites and economists such as David Ricardo almost two centuries ago. In response to Luddites smashing labor-saving textile machinery, Ricardo added the chapter "On Machinery" to the third (1821) edition of his *Principles of Political Economy and Taxation*, in which he allowed that the opinion prevailing in "the labouring class, that the employment of machinery is frequently detrimental to their interests, is not founded on prejudice and error, but is conformable to the correct principles of political economy" (p. 392). Most contemporary and subsequent economists strongly dissented.

Luddite arguments can be valid if an economy with less than full employment is "wage-led" in the sense that a higher real wage or wage share stimulates aggregate demand. In the short run, a lower labor/output ratio is unlikely to be followed immediately by a higher real wage, especially if some labor is unemployed. At the initial level of output, total wage payments will decline as jobs are eliminated, reducing consumer demand. If they are stimulated by demand pressure, investment and new capacity formation may also drop off. Is the unemployment it can cause a good reason to restrain the diffusion of labor-saving technical change? Before addressing this question directly, it makes sense to discuss the macroeconomic linkages between productivity growth and shifts in aggregate demand induced by a changing income distribution (see Rowthorn, 1982; Dutt, 1984; Taylor, 1991).

In an economy closed to foreign trade, an increase in the wage share has two immediate effects on aggregate demand: (1) if the propensity to consume from wage income exceeds the propensity from nonwage income (an econometric truism), then consumer demand will increase, possibly stimulating investment through the accelerator as well; (2) contrariwise, the corresponding reduction in the nonwage share may cut back on investment via reduced profitability. If the first effect dominates, then aggregate demand will increase with the wage share, or the economy can be called wage-led. By an obvious contrast, it becomes profit-led if the second effect is more important.

In an economy open to trade, further complications arise. One follows from the fact that the wage share, or the product of the real wage and the overall labor-output ratio, is a good approximation to labor costs per unit output. An increase in the share, therefore, may provoke higher export costs and a reduction in aggregate demand via falling sales abroad, i.e., an economy in which exports are cost-responsive is more likely to be profit-led.

The "Demand" curves in Figures 9.2 and 9.3 show capacity utilization (on the horizontal axes) increasing or decreasing as a function of unit labor cost (on the vertical axes) in the wage-led and profit-led

Figure 9.2 **Effects of Faster Productivity Growth when Effective Demand is Wage-led**

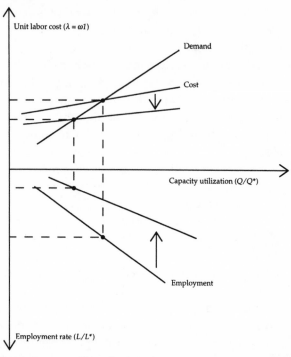

Note: Effects of more rapid productivity increases, which reduce the rate of growth of unit labor cost when aggregate demand is wage-led (the "Luddite case").

cases respectively. In the lower quadrants of both diagrams, the employment rate $L/\bar{L}$ * is an increasing function of capacity utilization $Q/\bar{Q}$ (the barred variables $\bar{L}$ and $\bar{Q}$ stand for "full" levels of employment and capacity use respectively).

The "Cost" schedules represent the supply side of the macroeconomic system, described in terms of steady states in which real unit labor cost λ = ωl is a constant (ω rises at the same percentage rate as l declines). As discussed in D.M. Gordon (1994) and Taylor (1991), bargaining between labor and management is likely to favor workers when the level of economic activity is high. That is, the cost schedules slope upward because real wages typically rise with output over the medium run.

As noted above, a speedup in productivity growth is not likely to be met by an increase in real wage growth immediately (econometric results suggest an elasticity in the vicinity of 0.5). Over time, however,

Figure 9.3 **Effects of Faster Productivity Growth when Effective Demand is Profit-led**

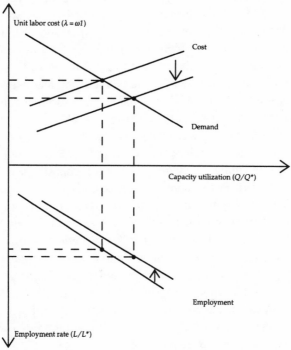

the wage will catch up, leading to a new steady state with constant but lower per unit labor costs—the downwardly shifted cost curves in Figures 9.2 and 9.3. In the lower quadrants of the diagrams, employment rates for given levels of capacity use (assumed to increase in the downward direction) will also be lower due to higher productivity — the "Employment" schedules shift inward.

In Figure 9.2, faster productivity growth leads to undesirable outcomes as a lower wage share causes aggregate demand to drop. There are reductions in the wage share, rate of capacity utilization, and employment rate. A wage-led economy is not well equipped to absorb technical advance. By contrast, the profit-led economy in Figure 9.3 ends up with higher capacity utilization and a stable employment rate because of the output increase caused by a strong investment and/or export response to lower unit costs.

In steady states when technical progress raises the productivity of labor only (the usual case), two further conditions apply: (1) the rate of growth of output will be the same as the rate of growth of the capital stock (both the rate of capacity utilization and the capital/capacity ratio are stable); and (2) the growth rate of employment will equal the difference between the growth rates of output and productivity. An obvious question is what happens to the capital stock (and output) growth rate in a new equilibrium like that of Figure 9.2?

To provide an answer, assumptions about the shape of the investment function are required. Two standard ones are that private capital formation responds negatively (but often weakly if the effect is observed at all) to higher unit labor costs as profitability declines, and positively to higher capacity utilization. In Figure 9.4, contour lines or loci of constant capital stock growth that incorporate these hypotheses are superimposed on the upper quadrant of Figure 9.2. Each dashed line in Figure 9.4 gives combinations of labor costs and levels of capacity utilization consistent with a constant capital growth rate, and lines farther to the right represent faster growth. The diagram shows steep iso-growth curves, corresponding to a much stronger output than profitability effect on investment demand (which helps give rise to a wage-led economy in the first place). It is easy to see that lower labor costs from faster productivity gains reduce the capital (and output) growth rate in the new steady state; employment growth also falls. The Luddite argument extends to the long run.

Does Figure 9.2 or Figure 9.3 apply in practice? The econometric results are not fully in, but available evidence suggests that aggregate demand tends to be profit-led in industrialized economies, and wage-led in developing countries. One clue is that in developing countries exchange rate devaluation, which cuts the real wage, often leads to reductions in output. The reverse appears to be the case in industrialized economies, with their more price-elastic export mix. Direct econometric evidence in support of profit-led adjustment in OECD countries is provided by Bowles and Boyer (1994) and D.M. Gordon (1994). For the developing countries, therefore, arguments in favor of limiting labor-saving technical change seem to make sense. However, this reasoning has a tremendous problem. Growth in real wages (and thereby real income per capita) is impossible without rising productivity; economies do not become prosperous on the basis of accumulation of physical and human capital alone. The operational question is not how to hold back productivity growth, but rather how to make it translate into higher real wages and aggregate demand.

Figure 9.4 **Effect of Faster Productivity Growth on the Growth Rate of Potential Output in the Wage-led Case**

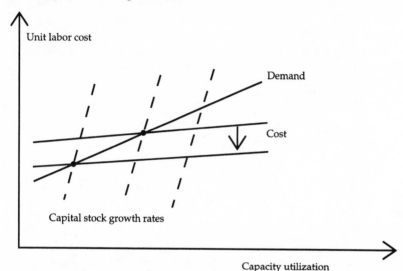

Capacity utilization

Note: Steady-state growth-reducing effect of faster productivity gains in a wage-led economy.

Inducing Productivity Growth

Higher investment, which would shift the whole family of iso-growth loci to the right, is one response to this challenge. As argued below, potential "crowding-in" effects of public on private capital formation can be crucial in this context, i.e., more public investment financed by progressive taxes is one means to attack the problems illustrated by Figures 9.2 and 9.4. Another option is an export push propelled by lower per unit costs. However, exports might also be induced by lower real wages as opposed to higher productivity. Which option is to be preferred?

The choices are illustrated in Figure 9.5. The rectangular hyperbolas in this diagram correspond to constant values of unit labor cost $\lambda = \omega l$; the "Low λ" schedule represents cheaper exports than "High λ." As the arrows illustrate, the economy can attain lower costs by either increasing productivity or cutting wages.

The East Asian "miracle" economies provide an intriguing contrast in this regard. In the 1950s, Hong Kong specialized in garment manufacture, with access to markets assured by the then lenient import

Figure 9.5 **Wage-cutting vs. Productivity Growth in Reducing Unit Labor Costs**

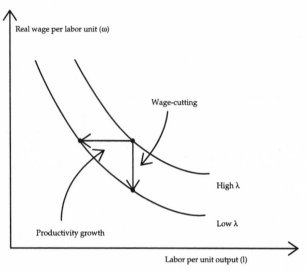

Note: Each rectangular hyperbola corresponds to a constant level of unit labor cost, $\lambda + \omega$, for different combinations of the real wage ω and the labor/output ratio l. Productivity growth reduces l and wage compression reduces ω, in different strategies aimed at increasing trade competitiveness by shifting to a lower unit labor cost curve.

quotas in the industrial economies. Its wages were low enough to give it cost advantages in cutting and sewing; for the first couple of decades, Hong Kong's rapid output growth was based squarely on cheap labor, its export markets "protected" from incursion by other producers by its preexisting quota rights. These structural features of the city-state's economy permitted its "free market" miracle to occur. In many respects, booming garment exports from South China in the 1980s represent a subsequent chapter of Hong Kong's economic history.

Unlike Hong Kong, Taiwan and South Korea initially specialized in textiles. Despite their status as "basket cases," these economies had wage levels that were *not* low enough to allow them to compete with Japan in world export markets. In terms of Figure 9.5, they had to cut wages or encourage productivity to get to "low λ" costs, which would enable them to undersell Japan. *Ex post*, it is clear they "chose" the high productivity road, negotiating it with heavily subsidized credit for local producers and hands-on industrial policy (see Amsden, Kochanowicz, and Taylor, 1994, chapter 4; Amsden, 1989; Chang, 1993).

The export-led expansion of output and employment in Korea and Taiwan had a distinctly non-laissez-faire character because their economies' initial structures made development unfold in *dirigiste* fashion, if it was to occur at all. Although side-by-side experiments will never be run, a sound historical judgment is that the "market" alone would never have generated the incentives required for Korean and Taiwanese enterprises to undertake drives for rapid productivity growth in manufacturing textiles. The state support they received strikingly contrasts with the sort of development strategies advocated for the last fifteen to twenty years by the World Bank (1991).

Employment Macroeconomics in Developing Countries

For developing economies less successful than those in East Asia, attaining adequate output and employment growth since the 1970s has been excruciatingly difficult. They have to deal not only with the longer-term difficulties just discussed, but also with macroeconomic adjustment problems centered around access to and effective use of hard currency. Following an old tradition in development economics, the constraints they face can be summarized in the form of "gaps" between available and desired levels of resources (Chenery and Bruno, 1962; Taylor, 1994b). They are put together here under the headings of saving, foreign exchange, and investment functions, which are deployed to analyze the policies poor countries can use to support output and employment when they are hit by external shocks. The options turn out to be limited, meaning that successful adjustment requires a more wide-ranging approach than is characteristic of current recommendations of agencies such as the World Bank and the International Monetary Fund.

The Saving Constraint

The first constraint comes from the national income and product accounts, reduced to a statement that investment must be financed by available saving. We can illustrate the forces that shift this relationship in a diagram with capacity utilization or employment on the horizontal axis and the rate of capacity growth or investment displayed vertically. The saving function itself is upward-sloping on the standard assumption that a fraction of any increase in output will be saved.

Changes in the rate of inflation are one important cause of movements of the saving schedule. Following the IMF's basic model as presented by Polak (1957), assume that the banking system is the economy's unique financial intermediary. A government deficit can be financed only by borrowing from banks, and the resulting monetary emission pushes prices up. Our first question is, what is the effect of faster inflation on the level of saving from a given income flow?

In old-fashioned monetarist language, the Fund's story is that the extra aggregate demand resulting from fiscal excess is self-financing via "inorganic emission" of money, which sets off inflation. The private sector may acquiesce for several reasons. One is that households are forced below their desired zero-inflation consumption level by supply preemption by the government. With access to bank loans, the government can use credit to get commodities, driving up prices as part of the process of crowding out consumption demand. A second reason is that there is an instantaneous loss in the real value of the existing money stock caused by the price increase induced by "printing" additional currency. The public may raise its saving to reconstitute wealth—rationally reducing demand to available supply. Third, faster inflation means that people need a bigger money stock for transactions purposes. With no easily liquifiable assets at hand, the only way they can build currency holdings up is to save more. On all counts, real consumption demand declines with faster inflation.

When the economy is wage-led, real wage cuts due to faster inflation will also reduce aggregate demand. If nominal wage increases are not fully indexed to rising prices, the real wage will fall. The national saving rate rises along the lines of Figures 9.2 and 9.4. This linkage was at least as important as the inflation tax in many developing economies in the 1980s. Real wage losses of 50 percent or more were observed in Latin American and African economies subject to massive external and supply shocks. Contrary to orthodox models, employment fell as well—there was a *positive* association between wages and employment as both collapsed. The conventional wisdom is that wage cuts will induce firms to hire more people, cutting unemployment and raising output at the same time.

Changes of external and fiscal balance can also influence overall saving. In principle, extra incoming foreign resources permit higher capital formation, shifting the national saving function up. But the increment may be well less than one-for-one due to capital flight and consumption leakages. Finally, as the IMF emphasizes, fiscal behavior matters. When public dissaving rises, then so must the inflation rate if overall saving is to be held constant.

The Foreign Exchange Constraint

The next accounting relationship is the foreign balance. It imposes an inverse or tradeoff relationship between short-term employment increases and investment for long-term growth, which has been acute in many developing economies.

The basic reason the tradeoff exists is that all economies apart from those of large, industrialized nations require imported capital goods. At the same time, intermediate imports are an essential input into current production in most developing economies, as a consequence of the pursuit of industrialization via import substitution. Increasing capacity utilization thus uses foreign exchange and crowds out capital formation.

In the 1980s, poor countries responded to this constraint in diverse fashion; e.g., Tanzania maintained 3 percent potential output growth while cutting capacity utilization by about 20 percent, while its neighbor Zimbabwe had negligible capacity growth but kept the level of activity high by directed import controls. In general, a bigger trade deficit permits higher imports of capital goods and thereby more investment, if output is held constant. This is *the* traditional two-gap argument à la Chenery and Bruno (1962).

The Investment Function

To construct a complete model, we have to add an investment function to the accounting already discussed. We assume that private investment responds to two key factors: One is public investment. Much recent evidence suggests that public investment has a net "crowding-in" effect on private capital formation. Creating infrastructure (think of irrigation projects) leads the private sector to undertake complementary projects. Public investment in manufacturing and public utilities can set up backward and forward linkages, as has long been recognized. Econometric results suggest that one dollar of public capital formation may induce a half-dollar or more worth of private projects.

The other factor driving capital formation is the level of economic activity. Both accelerator- and profitability-based investment theories

Figure 9.6 **A Three-gap Model**

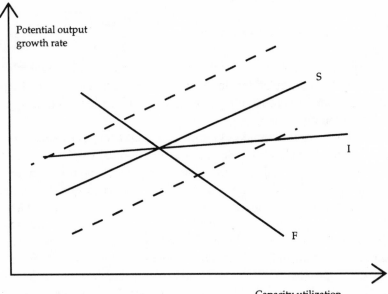

Note: Foreign exchange, investment, and saving schedules in a three-gap model. Dashed saving schedules represent different rates of inflation (higher toward the "northwest).

of the sort already discussed suggest a positive response of investment demand to higher output.

The Functions All Together

Figure 9.6 illustrates the model as stated so far in the capacity utilization vs. capacity growth rate plane. The saving (*S*), foreign exchange (*F*), and investment (*I*) schedules must cross in an equilibrium point. The inverse relationship between capacity utilization and potential output growth imposed by the external restriction shows up clearly, while investment is assumed to respond less strongly than saving to an increase in economic activity (a standard stability condition).

From the point of view of high school geometry, the obvious question about the diagram is what mechanisms permit *three* lines to cross in just one point? A couple of answers can be sketched out. One is that equilibrium is determined by the intersection of the saving and investment schedules as in traditional Keynesian macroeconomics. Via capital inflows and reserve changes, the foreign constraint shifts up or down to ratify this solution. Such a story is more characteristic of industrial economies and rapid growers such as the East Asian economies than it was of many foreign exchange constrained countries in the 1980s.

The other answer turns out to be inflation. Recall that the saving schedule was assumed to move upward with more rapidly rising prices, due to forced saving and the inflation tax. This mechanism generates a family of contour lines (or iso-inflation loci), with each curve giving the rate of potential output growth supported by saving as a function of capacity utilization at a constant inflation rate—the dashed lines illustrate two examples. Since faster inflation increases saving for a given level of output, contours farther to the northwest correspond to faster price increases.

The next question to ask is how does inflation get determined? As discussed by Kindleberger (1985) and Taylor (1991), two inflation theories have come down through more than two centuries of economic thought. One, conventionally called monetarist, postulates that inflation follows from money creation along the lines spelled out above. This theory goes together with a shifting saving function. Macro equilibrium is determined by the intersection of the foreign balance and investment schedule, and inflation varies to bring the saving schedule in line. An adverse foreign shock, which shifts the F-schedule downward, kicks off more inflation and lower employment, as observed in debtor countries in the 1980s.

The alternative, or structuralist, view is based on the input-output decomposition of the value of output into its component costs. Structuralists think that observed inflation reacts to increases in the nominal wage rate, the exchange rate, and other factors, including cost-push from increased charges for financing working capital when the interest rate rises and changes in flexible prices due to (for example) the evolution of food supply. This view says that the position of the saving function is fixed by the cost-driven inflation rate. Together with the investment curve, the S-schedule determines macro equilibrium, and the balance of payments has to adjust as discussed above.

The higher wisdom is that inflation in practice has both monetarist and structuralist roots, and we bear both in mind in the following discussion of macroeconomic adjustment problems.

Figure 9.7 **An Adverse External Shock in a Three-gap Model**

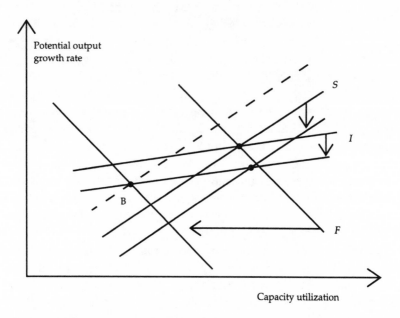

An Adverse External Shock

Figure 9.7 shows the impacts of an external shock, e.g., the large reduction in capital inflows for many countries in the wake of the debt crisis of 1982. The *F*-schedule shifts downward. With reduced external inflows, the rate of inflation has to rise to generate forced saving and a higher inflation tax to offset lower saving from abroad. That is, the whole family of *S*-curves shifts downward. Finally, credit conditions tighten, reducing investment demand.

A new demand-driven equilibrium in the diagram would correspond to the intersection of the shifted saving and investment schedules, with capital inflows adjusting. With a binding forex limit, such a Keynesian outcome at point A cannot be attained—the required level of imports simply cannot be paid for. Hence, real output tends toward B, where the investment and foreign schedules cross. In a monetarist adjustment scenario, the inflation rate would increase to ratify the (dashed) saving schedule passing through B, perhaps kicking off still higher rates of price and wage growth from the cost side.

An adequate policy response to an external shock is hard to orchestrate (Bacha, 1990). The shifting curves in Figure 9.7 suggest the following:

- Fiscal restraint will move the S-curves back to the left, permitting faster capacity growth and reduced inflation, but with lower capacity utilization and employment. Although it brings partial relief, austerity often is politically difficult to pursue.
- Increased public investment shifts the I-schedule up, speeding capacity growth when there is investment crowding in, at the cost of higher inflation and fewer jobs. Early in the 1980s, Brazil, South Korea, and Tanzania had some degree of success with this sort of policy.
- Higher exports can help release the forex limit. However, raising sales abroad in the short run can be difficult, especially for a raw material exporter. An export push is easier for semi-industrialized economies in which domestic recession creates spare manufacturing capacity that can be diverted to foreign markets, e.g., Turkey, Korea, or Brazil.
- Import quotas and controls can be used to change the slope and level of the F-schedule, permitting employment or investment to rise in conjunction with other policies. Tanzania, Zimbabwe, Kenya, and Colombia utilized variants of this option successfully in the 1980s.
- Policy coordination is never easy. Few developing (or developed!) country governments are agile enough to deploy simultaneous fiscal restraint in current transactions, increased state capital formation, intelligent manipulation of quotas, and export incentives to offset all the ill effects of an external shock. Certainly, the standard IMF package of demand restraint plus devaluation cannot restore the initial macro equilibrium in Figure 9.7. It is more likely to send investment and employment spiraling toward the southwest in a case of macroeconomic overkill.

Import Support and Other Inflows

In the early 1990s, foreign inflows to developing countries rose. There was renewed direct foreign investment in Latin America. African countries got aid for "import support" as local governments gained the local currency "counterpart" from sales of the foreign goods internally.

Figure 9.8 **A Favorable External Shock in a Three-gap Model**

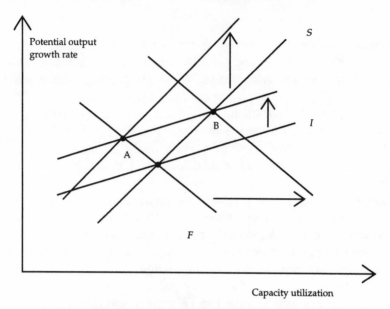

Note: Effects of an incoming foreign resource transfer.

It is straightforward to analyze possible responses to such flows in a gap framework.

Figure 9.8 illustrates responses to an increased foreign transfer. The *S*-curves shift upward, leading to lower output and slower capacity growth at a demand-determined equilibrium with the original rate of inflation, and the *F*-curve shifts outward. Investment may also rise (as shown) but does not have to. In the early 1990s many Latin American economies grew slowly even though they began to run trade deficits. In a gap setup, Ros (1992) shows how stagnant capital formation exacerbated by fiscal tightness and falling national saving as foreign money came in were major contributors to slow output growth.

Directed policy is needed to move the economy toward faster growth at point B. Slower inflation can shift the *S*-curves back to the right, reducing forced saving and the inflation tax. How rapidly such a transition can occur depends on the strength of cost pressures, including a potentially destabilizing speedup in inflation as employment rises. That is, an initial employment increase tends to bid up real wages, and aggregate demand in turn, if the economy is wage-led. The resulting additional output raises employment and wage pressure further still. Such feedbacks can directly destabilize real wage increases, or else can kick off inflation when production capacity limits begin to bind. Experience suggests that inflation may be difficult to control when extra spending power suddenly appears in the system from abroad, especially if the supply of key nontraded goods is relatively price-inelastic.

In these circumstances, relative prices of nontraded goods will rise when demand is generated by spending from inflows of foreign exchange. The disincentive effects on traded goods production and investment are called the Dutch disease in recent literature (in honor of natural gas revenues in The Netherlands), but the problem is endemic in developing countries with hard currency coming in from foreign aid or low-cost raw material exports. The disease can be a major barrier to job generation by industrialization—it is no accident that industry flourished in the East Asian economies bereft of natural resources.

More government dissaving also shifts the S-schedules to the right, as counterpart funds underwrite a boom led by public consumption. More sensible in the long run, perhaps, would be an increase in public investment, which would move the I-schedule upward, raising potential output growth but with faster inflation and lower capacity use.

In sum, absorption has to adjust to meet a higher foreign inflow, regardless of how external balance is reestablished. Part of that change would take the form of higher values of investment or employment, but exports may decline or additional imports come in. For these newly available goods to be absorbed in the market, either public or private consumption has to rise.

A more ominous possibility is capital flight, or an increase in forex sent abroad to finance increased external asset holdings by the private sector. When the higher initial foreign inflow goes to the government, then there has to be a public-to-private transfer to permit capital flight (the perhaps illegal obverse of the private-to-public transfer that debtor economies have to engineer). Imports have to be over-invoiced and exports under-invoiced or simply smuggled to generate capital outflows. These moves will be reflected in the national accounts by a decline in estimated national saving. Increased foreign inflows open channels for corruption both between the state and the private sector and in external trade.

Policy Implications

The policy bottom line is that maintaining employment levels and growth under macroeconomic conditions characteristic of developing countries is extremely difficult. Together with wage-led aggregate demand, the foreign exchange constraint imposes difficult tradeoffs between current output and capital formation. Even when external resources are available, directing the "foreign saving" that they represent into domestic capital formation is no easy task. An active public investment program is likely to be required. As we have seen, absorbing productivity growth in wage-led economies is tricky; they also face potentially destabilizing feedbacks between real wage increases and output expansion. An equable employment growth path can be very difficult to program—an unregulated market alone is not likely to turn the trick.

Problems with Stimulating Employment in Industrialized Economies

A similar comment applies to advanced economies, although the problems there stem more from internal distributional conflicts and instabilities in the capital account than from the current account of the balance of payments. (The following discussion draws heavily on D.M. Gordon, 1994, and Nell, 1994.)

Internal Distribution and Investment Demand

Figure 9.9 is a revised version of Figure 9.3, drawn to fit a high-income, profit-led economy. Note the nonlinearity in the "Cost" schedule, meaning that unit labor cost rises sharply at high levels of capacity utilization. The basic reason is a tighter labor market as output increases. The "cost of job loss" for employees declines, pushing up the profit-maximizing "efficiency wage" paid by employers. At the same time, the bargaining power of organized labor increases.

Figure 9.9 is also drawn with shallow capital stock growth rate schedules (the dashed lines). These contrast with the steep curves of Figure 9.4, signaling that investment in advanced economies responds

Figure 9.9 **A High Employment Profit Squeeze**

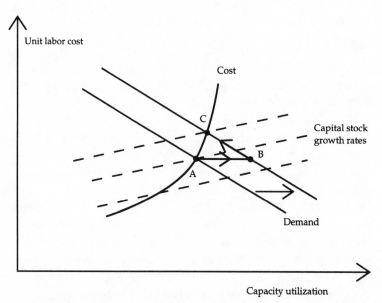

Note: Effects of expansionary policy. In this case in a profit-led (industrialized) economy with a high employment profit squeeze and investment highly sensitive to changes in profitability.

more strongly to profitability than to output changes. One reason often advanced is increased "globalization," meaning that firms have become sensitive to cross-border profit differentials in making their investment decisions. Also, more intense international competition in manufactured product markets means that higher unit labor costs will be reflected more rapidly into falling profits and therefore investment demand.

If these hypotheses are realistic, then sustained expansionary policy will not have strong effects on employment and can *reduce* growth, as shown by the shifting "Demand" schedule in Figure 9.9. In the short run, economic stimulus looks good, as output jumps from point A to point B and investment rises (B lies to the right of the capital stock growth curve running through A, meaning that higher capacity utilization stimulates investment demand). Over a longer period of time, however, the real wage and labor costs rise toward point C. The shallow capital stock growth rate curves signify that private investment will decline in reaction to a "high employment profit squeeze." The dynamic adjustment through points A, B, and toward C leads toward slower growth in the medium run.

There are further effects that can worsen these problems:

(1) The cost schedule may shift upward or become steeper, as higher observed wages feed back in positive, destabilizing fashion to labor militancy and still higher wage targets in contract negotiations (perhaps the case in the United States at the end of the 1970s).

(2) Both the demand schedule and the family of growth rate curves may shift downward due to other destabilizing feedback from reduced investment demand in the short run to dampened "animal spirits" at home and diversion of capital spending to projects abroad over the medium term.

(3) Such responses may be exacerbated if higher real wages and/or capacity utilization are associated with faster inflation. Combined with exogenous upward shifts in the cost schedule induced by the oil price shocks, such structuralist inflationary pressures triggered the staggering "anti-inflationary" interest rate hikes of the early 1980s. Tight money was anti-employment and curtailed investment spending.

(4) Widening trade deficits can also be associated with higher wages and employment, meaning that interest rates may also be increased to stanch external deficits. Alternatively, devaluation provokes further inflation. International capital movements that are highly responsive to interest rate differentials and expected exchange rate adjustments make the world financial system exquisitely sensitive to such signals.

Policy Binds

These problems go together across borders to tie the hands of all national policy makers. Although academic authors overrate the relevance of policy-related prisoners' dilemma games in which the players rationally choose not to cooperate, one may actually apply to the present international situation. Any single country that tries to expand is likely to suffer exchange appreciation resulting from the rising real wage of Figure 9.9, leading to falling net exports. Similarly, an attempt to lower interest rates will trigger capital flight. The expanding country risks losses that may loom large in terms of its internal political balance, while all its trading partners reap gains from higher exports and capital inflows. If countries were to expand together, all could gain, but then a nonexpanding "defector" would gain further still. The overall outcome is to bias each country's policy toward austerity.

This scenario is made more relevant by recent institutional developments. One is the growing importance of finance capital. Domestically, "financial deepening" goes with rising income. It means that the ratio of the value of inside financial assets to the value of real assets goes up; correspondingly, the political clout of financial as opposed to industrial capital will rise. The financial system can shift from concentrating on provision of productive credit either to preservation of financial wealth by high interest rates (the German case) or to facilitating speculative financial gains (the American savings-and-loan–junk-bond episode)—or both!

On the real side of the economy, rising cost schedules can also lead to political pressures for cutting wages as opposed to raising productivity along the lines of Figure 9.5. One interpretation of the British experiment under Conservative leadership runs exactly along these lines; perhaps the recent purchase of Rover by BMW signals the experiment's success. It remains to be seen, however, whether Britain is about to embark on a Hong Kong-like miracle of low-wage, export-led growth. If not, the harder path of raising productivity by public intervention may be the only option.

Policy Design

These considerations suggest that an effective employment policy package will need to have both national and international components. On the national side, they would include:

(1) public investment to shift upward the family of growth curves in Figure 9.9, raise private profitability, and speed productivity growth;

(2) intelligent macro policy, to dampen demand volatility and enhance job security, thus reducing real wage pressure and perhaps the high employment investment squeeze;

(3) nonorthodox moves such as price controls in case of inflationary bursts and directed industrial interventions (to design the latter, the traditional criteria of supporting branches with high-income elasticities of demand and good prospects for productivity growth

apply as well in industrial economies today as they did in East Asia in the 1950s and 1960s; Airbus is not the only recent success case);

(4) a policy of seeking productivity growth and new products, which is always preferable to cutting wages; but, as noted, adjusting to such changes is not always easy; so long as capitalist "progress" takes the forms illustrated in Figure 9.1, labor market adjustment policies and safety nets will have a social role to play.

Internationally, such policies would be complemented by restraints on production globalization and financial flows. With regard to the latter, any single country can impose a "stamp tax" on financial movements across its borders; the major financial centers together could impose a tax on all transactions. Since capital flows are price-sensitive, levies at modest rates might well dampen volume substantially and create more space for independent national policy.

There is also room for international coordination or—better—creation of income-sharing and support mechanisms to avoid the policy prisoners' dilemma sketched above. For example, their stockholders could push the Bretton Woods institutions in the direction of their original intent to support gradual accommodation of national economies to "structural" balance of payments surpluses and deficits (Dell, 1981). The Group of Seven countries might even agree to coordinated employment expansion together with restrictions on destabilizing financial flows, although recent history indicates that hopes for such action are probably in vain.

Indeed, the prisoners' dilemma over employment is not likely to be resolved until national political climates change. The "defect" or wage-cutting/austerity strategy in the game has dominated in recent decades precisely because upper-income groups in most industrialized nations have used it to reap substantial financial gains. Their political power, however, is not unlimited and groups that have lost ground are beginning to speak with a louder voice. The extent to which they are heard will determine whether policies that can aid employment growth and progressive income redistribution will really be put into place.

———— 10 ————

Reflections on a Sad State of Affairs

Robert Heilbroner

It is hard to know what is most disturbing about these trenchant essays: the distressing picture of the American economy that emerges from their pages; the dismaying inadequacy of the conventional economic diagnoses of, and remedies for, our difficulties; or the larger question of the problematic place of economics itself in today's rapidly restructuring world. I shall use this essay not to add to the empirical and analytical findings on which these issues rest, but to reflect on certain less clear-cut, but no less unsettling problems that they raise. Of necessity, these reflections must be generalizations, but I trust they will not be without cutting edges on that account.

The first reflection concerns the subject that binds these chapters—the persisting and sapping malfunctions of the American economy. These malfunctions begin with levels of unemployment that would have been judged unacceptable only a dozen or so years ago but are now regarded as "normal"; worse, given the near paranoid reaction of financial markets to the slightest hints of rising prices, they are considered desirable. Between 6 percent unemployment and 3 percent inflation, there is little doubt that the great preponderance of public, as well as political, opinion regards the former as the lesser evil. More distressing, one suspects that the majority of economists would concur.

As a number of essays have emphasized, however, our current malfunctions extend well beyond unemployment. The shrinking level of real incomes of the American working and middle classes; the deplorable erosion of work opportunities for the unskilled, largely black, members of society; and at a quite different level, the virtual disappearance of the oldest of national prerogatives—the ability to control the money supply to the degree needed to attain crucial national objectives—are also aspects of the general deterioration to which these re-flections will be directed.

Where to begin? I propose to start with a salient and yet insuffi-ciently appreciated fact. It is that most of the ills of the American economy can be found to a greater or lesser degree throughout the capitalist world. As John Eatwell makes clear at the outset, we are by no means the most severely afflicted economy in terms of unemployment. Indeed, all the G7 countries, excepting Japan and Germany, have per-formed worse than we. As with unemployment, so also with policy impotence: Wynne Godley recounts the complete inability of the Thatcher government to arrest the alarming deterioration of the British economy by means of conservative economic policies—an impasse mirrored to a lesser extent by the failure of the Mitterrand government to impart a forward momentum to the French economy with policies oriented more toward the left. A related resemblance lies in the deterio-ration of working- and lower-middle-class living standards about which David Gordon reports with respect to the United States. This, too, seems to be replicated abroad, even in Japan and Germany, the best-performing countries. Thus I suggest that an attempt to put into perspec-tive the situation in the United States must start from the recognition that not only has economic and social malfunction in our time become a generalized problem, but that its specific manifestations appear to be present, to a greater or lesser degree, in all advanced capitalist nations.

Can we explain this seemingly worldwide malfunction? I shall ven-ture the suggestion that its cause lies in a change in technology that has now become a strategic force in all advanced economies. The change lies in the congeries of advances we describe as automation. By auto-mation we mean the ability of "machines" to oversee the flow of production, to refine many aspects of the production flow while it is in progress, to test the ongoing accuracy of the manufacturing process, to supervise the levels of inventories needed as inputs and piling up as outputs, not to mention such matters as administering the payrolls, time sheets, and general paperwork that production generates. I have put the word *machines* between quotes because automation takes many forms, from the tiny chips that lie at the core of the new capabilities for self-guidance and self-correction, to the massive robots that perform the "work" of automated assembly lines. What interests us, however, are not these highly diverse technological advances but their common economic effect: automated production processes need much less directly applied labor, whether in the form of brute effort, routine calculation, or even experience-generated decision making, than did the processes of only twenty years ago. Automation assuredly creates new jobs and challenges as well, but they are located at the top of the employment pyramid, not at the bottom.

Here we see one direct relationship between the new technological aspect of our time and the widespread malfunctions that we set out to elucidate. The relation lies in the fact that, ceteris paribus, automation is unemployment-generating, at least to whatever extent it fails to give rise to second-order repercussions whose employment effect is positive. Alas, the two most powerful such effects worsen the immediate displacement of labor. The first of these is negative: automation is less expansive in its effects on overall investment than previous major technological advances, such as the railroad boom, the automotive boom, and most recently, the jet-plane boom, the single largest source of employment growth in the postwar period—tourism.

Why is automation less investment-generative than its precursors? The answer lies in the absence of a strategic attribute of earlier technological stimuli, namely their powerful inducements to create large new industrial salients. The railroad and automotive technologies brought not only investment in their own very extensive production facilities, but also the much larger public and private investment in the infrastructural needs to which they gave rise. So, too, the jet plane gave rise not only to the Boeing complex, and its smaller versions abroad, but to the airfields, hotels, and associated service facilities induced by mass air transportation. In a word, earlier technological advances typically brought into being entirely new sectors that rearranged the economic map with powerful employment-generating effects.

By way of contrast, automation has created no new second-order industries on anything approaching the scale of the past. To put it differently, yesterday's technology altered the landscape from without, while today's has changed it from within. Thus today's economic map appears much the same as did yesterday's. No major fields of consumption and investment have arisen to create a need for armies of labor. There have been, to be sure, new industrial salients, such as that connected with the generation of atomic power or space exploration, and there are innumerable computer repair and service small businesses, but these have been much too small to serve as transformational agencies, in Edward Nell's sense.

To this change in second-order effects, I now add another. Automative and computative technologies are more easily transplanted abroad than were the technologies of earlier revolutions, because they can be introduced into existing production processes rather than requiring the construction of whole new industries from the ground up. As a case in point, compare the arduous and lengthy importation of automobile manufacture into Japan after World War II with the very rapid automation of its automobile factories once they were built. Thus, the "penetrative" capability of the technology of automation explains much of the internationalization of production that has been such a destabilizing element in our period. Finally, an immensely powerful disruptive effect of automation has been its extraordinary enlargement of the capacity to amass and transmit information—the basis on which rests the unified world financial markets that have broken down the relatively insulated national monetary policies that were possible in a pre-electronic age.

I pass next to a matter that appears at first sight to be the very contrary of the search for an underlying causal unity to the malfunctions visible in so many capitalist nations. How can we account for the disparity of national performances in the face of a common underlying technological impetus? Japan, for example, has experienced less than half the percentage rise in unemployment of the United States. Germany has performed only marginally better than we have but would probably have far widened that margin had it not absorbed the East German economy, with its horrendous problems. Until recently, the Scandinavian trio also bettered U.S. performance.

Two explanations come to mind. The first concerns country-to-country variations in the institutional or sociopolitical constraints on, or encouragements to, performance: I think of such differences as the racial antagonisms that have impeded American growth, and their opposite, the cultural homogeneity that has long been a positive element in Scandinavian life; of differences in educational structures and traditions, where again the United States suffers in comparison to Germany, Japan, and Scandinavia; of obstacles to modernization lodged in special interest groups such as French agriculture, and in institutions that ease the adaptation to economic problems, like the labor-management arrangements in pre-unified Germany. Such constraints and encouragements exist in every country, where they play crucial roles in determining the effectiveness with which the forces of technological change can be managed.

The fact that no modern capitalist nation has been able wholly to insulate itself from the forces of technological change strongly implies that the protective effect of these institutional channels and barriers is limited—that technology "invades" all nations, both in the shape of employment-constraining change and intensified international involvement and exposure. At the same time, the differences in performance that we have noted certainly testify to some degree of effectiveness in constraining these forces across the international spectrum.

Why, then, are not the most effective means adopted by all nations? The answer brings us to the second explanation for variations in performance. It is that different institutions spring from, and embody, differing conceptions of the workings of a capitalist economy, which in turn leads to variations in the thrust of economic theorizing as noticeable across the spectrum of capitalisms as their institutional differences. I remind the reader of the existence of *dirigisme* in Mitterrand's France, *sozialmarktwirtschaft* in Germany, social welfarism in Sweden and Norway, and the unique configuration of "Japan Incorporated" during the same years that Thatcherism reigned in England and "supply-side" economics reigned in the United States. In brief, differences in sociopolitical premises powerfully affect the content of economic theory, which in turn leads to sharp differences in both the interpretation of events and the choice of responses to them. If a distinguished international committee of economists were to determine that a Japanese organization of industry, a Swedish trade union structure, and a German central banking system would best serve the American national interest, I do not think we could expect that their advice would be eagerly followed.

Thus, some part of the explanation for the variations in national performance can be traced to differences in pre-analytic "vision," from which flow differences in economic policy. An interesting example here is the unraveling of the Keynesian consensus that occurred in the United States during the 1970s and 1980s, mainly as a consequence of the failure of Keynesian economics to anticipate inflation. A number of competing theoretical approaches sprang up, among them rational expectations, monetarism, new classical and new Keynesian economics, none of which ever achieved the consensus that Keynesianism had once enjoyed, but all sharing a distaste for the active fiscalism that sprang from Keynes's central placement of uncertainty and lurking instability (see Heilbroner and Milberg, 1996).

The striking shift in American economic policy from the interventionism of the Kennedy-Johnson years to the much more passive stance of the Reagan-Bush days can likely be attributed, at least to a considerable degree, to this shift in the vision of the workings of the system. It should also be noted in this context that the anti-Keynesian movement never gained a similar importance in Europe, where Keynesianism itself had never sunk its roots as deeply as in the United States—a state of affairs that undoubtedly played its part in the more interventionist policies of other G7 nations, England excepted.

This now introduces us to the third of the larger issues to which this final chapter is addressed: the extraordinary doubts that are raised with respect to the efficacy of economic policy itself by the challenges and uncertainties of our time of troubles.

Here two issues again come to the fore. The first is whether it is possible to assess the comparative effectiveness of economic policy—and, of course, its underlying theory—given the differences in institutional settings among nations. Can one, for example, put forward a general assessment of a policy such as NAFTA, when its consequences are likely to be strikingly different in a nation that takes strong measures to relocate and retrain workers threatened by an influx of imports, compared with another that actively practices a laissez-faire attitude with respect to the same influx? In the same fashion, will not the acceptable tradeoff between unemployment and inflation be differently appraised in countries with differing unemployment insurance systems, and will not wage-squeeze stagnation be accorded very different receptions in nations with strong or weak union structures?

In other words, variances in sociopolitical constraints make it exceedingly difficult to declare with certainty whether the success or failure of a given policy is the consequence of its theoretical validity or its institutional setting. This has always been the case to some extent, but the problem is compounded by a difficulty to which reference has been made above. That is the absence, especially in this country, of a consensual unity of views about economic theory, which implies an underlying absence of consensus about the sociopolitical belief systems from which economic policy ultimately springs. When doctors do not come to common diagnoses, confidence in their suggested remedies declines. Thus, one reason that the confidence reposed in economics seems to me at a low ebb is that we lack the confidence once bestowed by Keynesian doctrine, and before that by Marshallian, and still earlier by Millian, Ricardian, and Smithian views.

To that general description, it is necessary to add a word regarding a peculiar ailment that appears to afflict the economics practiced in contemporary America. This is its indifference to matters of practical importance when they challenge the conceptual basis on which economic theory is raised. I content myself with a few examples: it is a serious misrepresentation of economic realities when the conventional national accounts treat all government expenditure as the equivalent of consumption, but this is nonetheless the manner in which public expenditure is represented. When economic teaching has forgotten about John Stuart Mill's distinction between "productive" consumption expenditure that renews the body social and "unproductive" consumption that has no such effect, it gravely weakens our capacity to judge whether or not rising consumption is a sign of increasing well-being. When the doctrine of free trade is presumed from the outset to produce full employment, without consideration of the mobility of labor and capital, it endorses a national policy that may, in actuality, produce effects very different from those that have been confidently anticipated. When the goal of public finance is a zero deficit, that means no more Panama Canals. When the fundamental building block of economic theory is taken to be "the individual," it passes over the awkward question of how such a monad can receive "income" except from another individual, in which case the fundamental building block must be a dyad, which is the gene of a society. When the study of institutional and ideological differences, such as those I have outlined, is considered to be a matter for "sociology" but hardly for serious economic inquiry, it is not surprising that economics becomes an unreliable—worse, an untrustworthy—discipline.

It is not, fortunately, irremediably so. The sharp edge and strong pragmatic tone of the essays in this collection attest to the possibility of breathing new life into economics, a life sorely needed in a nation that must run the gauntlet of a new technological age at the same time that the established structure of world order is in a condition of upheaval. Economics cannot be the sole radar by which we safely find our way through this difficult state of affairs. Even at its best it will be an unreliable instrument of navigation unless it is placed alongside a trustworthy compass of social responsibilities, a reliable depth gauge of political sentiments, and a strong beacon light of moral conviction. Put differently, economic reasoning is necessary, but not sufficient, for a safe passage during the decades ahead. I would like to think that these essays, with their institutional sensitivity, their conceptual pragmatism, and their political candor, might serve as a model for the work that economics can do in the future.

Bibliography

Abernathy, W., and Hayes, R. 1980. "Managing Our Way to Economic Decline." *Harvard Business Review* (July/August).

Abramovitz, M. 1986. "Catching Up, Forging Ahead, and Falling Behind." *Journal of Economic History* 46.

Abramovitz. M. 1994. "Catching Up." In Baumol, Nelson, and Wolff 1994.

Aizenman, J. 1986. "Testing Deviations from Purchasing Power Parity." *Journal of International Money and Finance* 5: 25–35.

Allen, W. R., ed. 1967. *International Trade Theory: Hume to Ohlin*. New York: Random House.

Amsden, A.H. 1989. *Asia's Next Giant*. New York: Oxford University Press.

Amsden, A.H. 1991. "The Diffusion of Development: The Late Industrialization Model and Greater East Asia." *American Economic Review* 81.

Amsden, A.H.; Kochanowicz, J.; and Taylor, L. 1994. *The Market Meets Its Match: Restructuring the Economies of Eastern Europe*. Cambridge, Mass.: Harvard University Press.

Arndt, S.W., and Richardson, J.D., eds. 1987. *Real-Financial Linkages among Open Economies*. Cambridge, Mass: MIT Press.

Aschauer, D. 1990. *Public Investment and Private Sector Growth*. Washington, D.C.: Economic Policy Institute.

Bacha, E.L. 1990. "A Three-Gap Model of Foreign Transfers and the GDP Growth Rate in Developing Countries." *Journal of Development Economics* 32: 279–96.

Barro, R.J. 1976. "Rational Expectations and the Role of Money." *Journal of Monetary Economics* 2.

Barro, R.J. 1977. "Unanticipated Monetary Growth and Unemployment in the United States." *American Economic Review* 67 (March).

Barro, R.J. 1984. *Macroeconomics*. New York: John Wiley.

Bartlett, C.A., and Ghoshal, S. 1989. *Managing Across Borders: The Transnational Solution*. Boston, Mass.: Harvard Business School Press.

Baumol, W.J.; Nelson, R.R.; and Wolff, E.N., eds. 1994. *Convergence of Productivity: Cross-National and Historical Evidence*. New York: Oxford University Press.

Beveridge, W.H. 1944. *Full Employment in a Free Society*. London: Allen and Unwin.

Bienenfeld, M. 1988. "Regularities in Price Changes as an Effect of Changes in Distribution." *Cambridge Journal of Economics* 12, no. 2 (June): 247–55.

Bowles, S., and Boyer, R. 1995. "Wages, Aggregate Demand, and Employment in an Open Economy: A Theoretical and Empirical Investigation." In Epstein and Gintis forthcoming.

Bowles, S.; Gordon, D.M.; and Weisskopf, T.E. 1989. "Business Ascendancy and

Economic Impasse: A Structural Retrospective on Conservative Economics, 1979–87." *Journal of Economic Perspectives.*

Bowles, S.; Gordon, D.M.; and Weisskopf, T.E. 1990. *After the Waste Land: A Democratic Economics for the Year 2000.* Armonk, N.Y.: M.E. Sharpe.

Business Week, "Jobs, Jobs, Jobs," February 22, 1993.

Chandler, A.D., Jr. 1990. *Scale and Scope: The Dynamics of Industrial Capitalism.* Cambridge, Mass.: Harvard University Press.

Chang, H.-J. 1993. "The Political Economy of Industrial Policy in Korea." *Cambridge Journal of Economics* 17: 131–57.

Chenery, H.B., and Bruno, M. 1962. "Development Alternatives in an Open Economy: The Case of Israel." *Economic Journal* 72: 79–103.

Chrystal, K. A., and Sedgwick, R. 1989. "Exchange Rates and Open Economy Macroeconomics: An Introduction." In *Exchange Rate and Open Economy Macroeconomics*, R. MacDonald and M.P. Taylor, eds. Oxford: Basil Blackwell.

Crouhy-Veyrac, L., and Crouhy, M. and J. Mélitz. 1982. "More about the Law of One Price." *European Economic Review* 18: 325–44.

Dell, S. 1981. *On Being Grandmotherly: The Evolution of IMF Conditionality.* Essays on International Finance no. 141. Princeton, N.J.: Princeton University Press.

Dernburg, T.F. 1989. *Global Macroeconomics.* New York: Harper and Row.

Dollar, D.; Wolff, E.; and Baumol, W. 1988. "The Factor Price Equalization Model and Industry Labor Productivity: An Empirical Test across Countries." In *Empirical Methods for International Trade*, Robert C. Feenstra, ed. Cambridge, Mass.: MIT Press.

Dore, R. 1973. *British Factory–Japanese Factory: The Origins of National Diversity in Industrial Relations.* Berkeley: University of California Press.

Dornbusch, R. 1988. *Real Exchange Rates and Macroeconomics: A Selective Survey.* NBER Working Paper no. 2775. Cambridge, Mass.

Dosi, G.; Pavitt, K.; and Soete, L. 1990. *The Economics of Technical Change and International Trade.* New York: New York University Press.

Dutt, A.K. 1984. "Stagnation, Income Distribution, and Monopoly Power." *Cambridge Journal of Economics* 8: 25–40.

Eatwell, J. 1994a. "The Coordination of Macroeconomic Policy in the European Community." In J. Michie and J. Grieve Smith 1994.

Eatwell, J. 1994b. "Coordination Failure." *New Economy* (September).

Eisner, R. 1986. *How Real Is the Federal Deficit?* New York: Free Press.

Epstein, G., and Gintis, H., eds. Forthcoming. *The Political Economy of Investment, Saving, and Finance: A Global Perspective.* Cambridge: Cambridge University Press.

Emmanuel, A. 1972. *Unequal Exchange.* New York: Monthly Review Press.

Executive Office of the President. 1993. *Economic Report of the President.* Washington, D.C.: U.S. Government Printing Office.

Fagerberg, I. 1988. "Why Growth Rates Differ." In *Technical Change and Economic Theory*, G. Dosi et al., eds. London: Pinter.

Faux, J., and Lee, T. 1993. *The Effects of George Bush's NAFTA on American Workers: Ladder Up or Ladder Down?* Briefing Paper. Washington, D.C.: Economic Policy Institute.

Feldstein, M. 1993. *The Dollar and the Trade Deficit in the 1980's.* NBER Working Paper no. 4325. Cambridge, Mass.

Flaherty, M.-Th. 1986. "Coordinating International Manufacturing and Technology." In M.E. Porter 1986.

Frenkel, J.A. 1978. "A Monetary Approach to the Exchange Rate: Doctrinal Aspects and Empirical Evidence." In *The Economics of Exchange Rates*, J.A. Frenkel and H.G. Johnson, eds. Reading, Mass.: Addison-Wesley.

Friedman, M. 1968. "The Role of Monetary Policy." *American Economic Review* 58.

Gerschenkron, A. 1962. *Economic Backwardness in Historical Perspective*. Cambridge, Mass.: Harvard University Press.

Ghemawat, P.; Porter, M.E.; and Rawlinson, R.A. 1986. "Patterns of International Coalition Activity." In M.E. Porter, ed., 1986.

Giovannini, A. 1988. "Exchange Rates and Traded Goods Prices." *Journal of International Economics* 24: 45–68.

Glyn, A.; Hughes, A.; Lipietz, A.; and Singh, A. 1990. "The Rise and Fall of the Golden Age." In Marglin and Schor 1990.

Gordon, D.M. 1972. *Theories of Poverty and Underemployment*. Lexington, Mass.: Lexington Books.

Gordon, D.M. 1977. "Counting the Underemployed." In *Problems in Political Economy: An Urban Perspective*, D.M. Gordon, ed. Lexington, Mass.: D.C. Heath.

Gordon, D.M. 1987. "Six-Percent Unemployment Ain't Natural: Demystifying the Idea of a Rising 'Natural Rate of Unemployment'." *Social Research* 54, no. 2 (Summer).

Gordon, D.M. 1988. "The Un-natural Rate of Unemployment: An Econometric Critique of the NAIRU Hypothesis." *American Economic Review* 78, no. 2 (May).

Gordon, D.M. 1993. "Clintonomics: A Glass Half Empty." *Contention*.

Gordon, D.M. 1995. "Growth, Distribution and the Rules of the Game: Social Structuralist Macro-Foundations for a Democratic Economic Policy." In Epstein and Gintis forthcoming.

Gordon, R.J. 1979. "The 'End-of-Expansion' Phenomenon in Short-Run Productivity Behavior." *Brookings Papers on Economic Activity*.

Gordon, R.J. 1993. "The Jobless Recovery: Does It Signal a New Era of Productivity-Led Growth." *Brookings Papers on Economic Activity*.

Hamermesh, D., and Grant, J. 1979. "Econometric Studies of Labor-Labor Substitution and Their Implications for Policy." *Journal of Human Resources*.

Harrod, R. 1933. *International Economics*. Chicago: University of Chicago Press (revised edition, 1957).

Heilbroner, R., and Milberg, W. 1996. *The Crisis of Vision in Modern Economic Thought*. New York: Cambridge University Press.

Hikino, T., and Amsden, A.H. 1994. "Staying Behind, Stumbling Back, Sneaking Up, Soaring Ahead: Late-Industrialization in Historical Perspective." In Baumol, Nelson, Wolff 1994.

Itoh, M.; Kiyono, K.; Okuno-Fugiwara, M.; and Suzumura, K. 1991. *Economic Analysis of Industrial Policy*. San Diego: Academic Press.

Johnson, C. 1982. *MITI and the Japanese Miracle: The Growth of Industrial Policy, 1925–1975*. Stanford, Calif.: Stanford University Press.

JEC (Joint Economic Committee), Congress of the United States. 1993a. *The 1993 Joint Economic Report*. Washington, D.C.

JEC (Joint Economic Committee), Congress of the United States. 1993b. *Potential Economic Impact of NAFTA: An Assessment of the Debate.* Staff Study, October. Washington, D.C.

"Kaldor's Growth Laws," Symposium. 1983. *Journal of Post-Keynesian Economics* 3 (Spring).

Keynes, J.M. 1936. *The General Theory of Employment, Interest, and Money.* London: Macmillan.

Kindleberger, C.P. 1985. *Keynesianism vs. Monetarism and Other Essays in Financial History.* London: Allen and Unwin.

Kitson, M., and Michie, J. 1994. "Depression and Recovery, Lessons from the Interwar Period." In Michie and Smith 1994.

Koechlin, T.; Larudee, M.; Bowles, S.; and Epstein, G. 1993. *Effect of the North American Free Trade Agreement on Investment, Employment and Wages in Mexico and the United States.* Working Paper, Department of Economics, University of Massachusetts, Amherst, Mass.

Kravis, I.B., and Lipsey, R.E. 1987. "The Assessment of National Price Levels." In Arndt and Richardson 1987.

Krueger, A.O. 1983. *Exchange-Rate Determination.* Cambridge, Mass: Cambridge University Press.

Leontief, W. 1985. *Essays in Economics.* Armonk, N.Y.: M.E. Sharpe.

Levich, R.M. 1985. "Empirical Studies of Exchange Rates: Price Behavior, Rate Determination and Market Efficiency." *Handbook of International Economics,* vol. 2. Amsterdam: Elsevier.

Lucas, R.E., Jr. 1973. "Some International Evidence on Output-Inflation Tradeoffs." *American Economic Review* 63.

Maddison, A. 1982. *Phases of Capitalist Development.* Oxford: Oxford University Press.

Maddison, A. 1991. *Dynamic Forces in Capitalist Development: A Long-Run Comparative View.* New York: Oxford University Press.

Mansfield, E. 1968. *The Economics of Technological Change.* New York: W.W. Norton.

Marglin, S., and Schor, J., eds. 1990. *The Golden Age of Capitalism,* Oxford: Oxford University Press.

Marston, R.C. 1987. "Real Exchange Rates and Productivity Growth in the United States and Japan." In Arndt and Richardson 1987.

Mataloni, R., Jr. 1993. "U.S. Multinational Companies: Operations in 1991." *Survey of Current Business* (July).

McCloskey, D.N., and Zecher, J.R. 1985. "How the Gold Standard Worked, 1880–1913." In *The Gold Standard in History and Theory,* B. Eichengreen, ed. New York: Methuen.

Michie, J., and Smith, J.G., eds. 1994. *Unemployment in Europe.* London: Academic Press.

Milberg, W., and Elmslie, B. 1992. "Technical Change in the Corporate Economy: A Vertically Integrated Approach." In *The Megacorp and Macrodynamics,* W. Milberg, ed. Armonk, N.Y.: M.E. Sharpe.

Moore, B.J. 1988. *Horizontalists and Verticalists: The Macroeconomics of Credit Money.* Cambridge: Cambridge University Press.

Munnell, A. 1990. "Why Has Productivity Growth Declined? Productivity and

Public Investment. *New England Economic Review* (January–February).

Nasdone, T.; Herz, D.; Mellor, E.; and Hipple, S. 1992. "Job Market in the Doldrums." *Monthly Labor Review* (February).

Nell, E. 1988. *Prosperity and Public Spending*. Boston: Unwin Hyman.

Nell, E. 1992. *Transformational Growth and Effective Demand*. New York: New York University Press.

Nell, E. 1994. *Unemployment, Aggregate Demand, and Government Policy*, mimeo, New York: New School for Social Research.

Nelson, R.R. 1991. "Diffusion of Development: Post-World War II Convergence among Advanced Industrial Nations." *American Economic Review* 81, no. 2 (May).

Ochoa, E. 1988. "Values, Prices, and Wage-Profit Curves in the U.S. Economy." *Cambridge Journal of Economics* 13: 413–30.

OECD. 1993. *Economic Survey: United States*. Paris: OECD.

Officer, L.H. 1976. "The Purchasing Power Parity Theory of Exchange Rates: A Review Article." *IMF Staff Papers*, March.

Palley, T.I. 1993. "The Duration Phillips Curve: Theory and Evidence." Unpublished manuscript.

Palley, T.I. 1994. "Escalators and Elevators: A Phillips Curve for Keynesians." *Scandinavian Journal of Economics*.

Pasinetti, L.L. 1981. *Structural Change and Economic Growth*. Cambridge: Cambridge University Press.

Patel, P., and Pavitt, K. 1991. "Europe's Technological Performance." In *Technology and the Future of Europe: Global Competition and the Environment in the 1990s*, C. Freeman et al., eds. London: Pinter.

Peterson, P. 1994. *Facing Up: How to Rescue the Economy from Crushing Debt and Restore the American Dream*. New York: Simon & Schuster.

Peterson, W. 1994. *Silent Depression*. New York: W.W. Norton.

Phelps, E. 1967. "Money Wage Dynamics and Labor Market Equilibrium." *Journal of Political Economy* (July-August).

Polak, J.J. 1957. "Monetary Analysis of Income Formation and Payments Problems." *International Monetary Fund Staff Papers* 1: 1–50.

Porter, M.E., ed. 1986. *Competition in Global Industries*. Boston, Mass.: Harvard Business School Press.

Porter, M.E., and Fuller, M.B. 1986. "Coalitions and Global Strategy." In M.E. Porter 1986.

Protopapadakis, A.A., and Stoll, H.R. 1986. "The Law of One Price in International Commodity Markets: A Reformulation and Some Formal Tests." *Journal of International Money and Finance* 5: 335–60.

Ricardo, D. [1817] 1951. *Principles of Political Economy and Taxation*, P. Sraffa, ed. Cambridge: Cambridge University Press.

Ros, J. 1992. *Foreign Exchange and Fiscal Constraints on Growth*, mimeo, Notre Dame, Ind.: University of Notre Dame.

Rowthorn, R. 1982. "Demand, Real Wages, and Economic Growth." *Studi Economici* 18: 2–53.

Rueff, J. 1967. *The Balance of Payments*. New York: Macmillan.

Scherer, F.M., and Ross. D. 1990. *Industrial Market Structure and Economic Performance*. Dallas, Texas: Houghton Mifflin.

Schonberger, R.J. 1982. *Japanese Manufacturing Techniques: Nine Hidden Lessons in Simplicity.* New York: Free Press.

Schor, J.B. 1991. *The Overworked American: The Unexpected Decline of Leisure.* New York: Basic Books.

Schumpeter, J.A. 1954. *History of Economic Analysis.* Oxford: Oxford University Press.

Semmler, W. 1984. *Competition, Monopoly, and Differential Profit Rates.* New York: Columbia University Press.

Shaikh, A. 1980. "On the Laws of International Exchange." In *Growth, Profits and Property: Essays in the Revival of Political Economy,* E.J. Nell, ed. Cambridge: Cambridge University Press.

Shaikh, A. 1984. "The Transformation from Marx to Sraffa: Prelude to a Critique of the Neo-Ricardians." In *Marx, Ricardo, Sraffa,* E. Mandel, ed. London: Verso.

Shaikh, A. 1991. *Competition and Exchange Rates: Theory and Empirical Evidence.* Working Paper no. 25. New York: New School for Social Research.

Sharp, M. 1993. "Industrial Policy in a Global Environment." In *New Challenges to International Cooperation: Adjustment of Firms, Policies and Organizations to Global Competition,* P. Gourevitch and P. Guerrieri, eds. San Diego: University of California, International Relations and Pacific Studies.

Shonfield, A. 1965. *Modern Capitalism: The Changing Balance of Public and Private Power.* London: Oxford University Press.

Soete, L., and Dosi, G. 1983. *Technological Trends and Employment, Electronics and Communications.* London: Gower.

Stanford, J. 1993. "Continental Economic Integration: Modeling the Impact on Labor." *Annals of the American Academy.*

Summers, L.H. 1983. "The Nonadjustment of Nominal Interest Rates: A Study of the Fisher Effect." In *Macroeconomics, Prices, and Quantities: Essays in Memory of Arthur M. Okun,* J. Tobin, ed. Washington, D.C.: Brookings Institution.

Taylor, L. 1991. *Income Distribution, Inflation, and Growth.* Cambridge, Mass.: MIT Press.

Taylor, L. 1994a. "Pasinetti's Processes." *Cambridge Journal of Economics.*

Taylor, L. 1994b. "Gap Models." *Journal of Development Economics.*

Temin, P. 1989. *Lessons from the Great Depression.* Cambridge, Mass.: MIT Press.

Tobin, J. 1972. "Inflation and Unemployment." *American Economic Review 62.*

Uimonen, P. 1993. *Public Debt, Public Investment and Productivity Growth.* Ph.D. dissertation, New York: New School for Social Research.

UNCTC (United Nations Centre on Transnational Corporations). 1990. *New Approaches to Best-Practice Manufacturing: The Role of Transnational Corporations and Implications for Developing Countries.* Series A, no. 12. New York: United Nations.

UNCTAD (United Nations Conference on Trade and Development). 1987. *Trade and Development Report, 1987.* Geneva: United Nations.

UNPTC (United Nations Programme on Transnational Corporations). 1993. *World Investment Report 1993: Transnational Corporations and Integrated International Production.* New York: United Nations.

U.S. Bureau of Labor Statistics. *Bulletins* 1118, 2033, 2104, 2182, 2242, 2263, 2316, 2367. Washington, D.C.: U.S. Government Printing Office.

U.S. Bureau of Labor Statistics. 1988. *Labor Force Statistics Derived from the Current Population Surveys.* Bulletin no. 2307. Washington, D.C.: U.S. Government Printing Office.

U.S. Bureau of Labor Statistics. 1993. *Employment and Earnings.* December. Washington, D.C.: U.S. Government Printing Office.

U.S. Department of Commerce. 1993. *Survey of Current Business.* December. Washington, D.C.: U.S. Government Printing Office.

Vernon, R. 1966. "International Investment and International Trade in the Product Cycle." *Quarterly Journal of Economics.*

Wood, A.J.B. 1994. *North-South Trade, Employment and Inequality: Changing Fortunes in a Skill-Driven World.* Oxford: Clarendon Press.

World Bank. 1991. *World Development Report.* New York: Oxford University Press.

Wray, L.R. 1990. *Money and Credit in Capitalist Economies: The Endogenous Money Approach.* Aldershot, Hants, England: Edward Elgar.

Zeile, W.J. 1993. "Merchandise Trade of U.S. Affiliates of Foreign Companies." *Survey of Current Business* (October).

Index

A

Absolute costs, 60, 67, 77
African-Americans, 79
Aggregate demand, 109–35, 145, 148
  components of, 117–29
  and construction, 121–23
  consumption, 118–20
  and government spending, 124–25,
    126–29, 132–33
  and investment, 120–21
  and net exports, 123–24
  policy implications of, 132–35
  and taxation and deficit, 125–26
  and wage cuts, 160
  and wage share, 153–55
Austerity, 75, 130, 160, 171
  reasons for, 116–17
Automatic stabilizers, 110, 124
Automation, 174–76
Automobiles, 124

B

Balance of trade, 75
Bartlett, C.A., 53
Benefits, employee, 105
Beveridge, William, 137
Bretton Woods system, 10–11, 14, 17,
  64, 116
Brittan, Samuel, 22–23
Bundesbank, 16
Business-cycle peaks, 91

C

Canada, 66, 77
Capacity utilization, 111, 153–55, 162

Capital
finance, 171
flight, 167
flows, 172
and exchange rates, 63
formation, 156, 161
Capital goods
  cost of, 80–82
  growth rates for, 83
  and unskilled labor, 82–84
Coalitions, 57
Colleges, 84
Commodity points, 69–70
Comparative costs, 61, 67, 68
Computers, 124
Construction, 121–23
Consumer demand, 153
Consumption, 118–20
  and investment, 122
  productive versus unproductive, 179
Convergence, 41–42, 45, 47–51, 57–58
Credibility, 12–13
Credit, 34, 38
Currency
  devaluation, 68
  money supply, 110
  See also Exchange rates

D

Deficit spending, 125, 160
Demand, 6–7
  growth slowdown, 8–14
  management theory, 124
  saturation, 151
  See also Aggregate demand;
    Consumer demand

Democratic policies, 114–16
Deregulation, financial system, 11
Discouraged workers, 111
Dornbusch, R., 64
Draft, military, 120
Durables, 119, 124

E

Economic Report of the President,
    140–41
Education, 84
Efficiency, 60
Elasticities problem, 68
Employment
  in developing countries, 159–63
  foreign exchange constraint, 161,
    162–63
  impact of adverse shocks on, 164–
    65
  and import support, 165–67
  investment function, 161–63
  policies for, 168
  savings constraint on, 159–61,
    162–63
  direct programs for, 85
  growth,
  international cooperation for, 172
  labor payments and costs, 152–5
    6
  in long run, 148–59
  and productivity growth, 157–59
  realization and disproportionality
    problems, 149–52
  stimulating global, 147–72
  and technology, 41–43
  in industrialized economies, 168–
    72
  internal distribution and investment
    demand, 168–70
  policy binds for, 170–71
  policy design, 171–72
  See also Full employment; Labor;
    Unemployment; Wages
England. *See* Great Britain

Europe
  labor shortage in, 8
  white-colar unemployment in, 58
  See also specific countries
European Common Market, 77
European Community trade balances,
    15
European Monetary System, 10–11
European Union
  external balance of, 17
  full employment strategy for, 16–18
Exchange Rate Mechanism (ERM), 10
Exchange rates, 8, 10–11, 14–16
  and austerity measures, 116
  and developing country
    employment, 161
  in European Union, 16
  fixed, 63–64
  flexible, 64
  and free trade, 61–62
  in Great Britain, 19–20
  and inflation, 73–74
  and international capital flows, 63
  and international trade, 61–62, 72–74
  manipulation of, 59
  risk privatization of, 11
  speculation in, 10–12
  and unit labor costs, 72
Export push, 160

F

Federal Civil Works Administration
    (FCWA), 85
Financial instability, 13–14
Financial system deregulation, 11
Fiscal policy, 139, 145–46
France, 8, 174, 176
Free markets, 134–35
Free trade. *See* Trade
Free Trade Agreement (FTA), 66,
    76
Friedman, Milton, 27, 140
FTA. *See* Free Trade Agreement

Full employment
  changing measures of, 141
  defined, 137
  economists and retreat from, 138–41
  for European Union, 16–18
  and free trade, 61
  and inflation constraint, 137–46
  and labor productivity, 147
  macroeconomic consistency
    conditions for, 149–52
  policy for, 14–16
  in Great Britain, 18–20
Full Employment in a Free Society
  (Beveridge), 137
Fuller, Mark, 57

G

GATT. *See* General Agreement on
  Tariffs and Trade
General Agreement on Tariffs and
  Trade (GATT), 58, 85
General Theory (Keynes), 12, 139
Germany, 6, 8, 14, 174, 176
Gerschenkron, Alexander, 49–50
Ghoshal, S., 53
Gold standard, 18
Goods. *See* Capital goods; Durables
Gordon, Robert J., 89
Great Britain, 17, 21–40, 110, 171, 174
  austerity measures in, 116
  balance of payments in, 38, 39, 40
  competitive capacity in, 18–19
  consumer boom in, 34, 36
  debt increase in, 34, 35, 36, 38
  deflationary budget of, 32
  full employment policy for, 18–20
  income distribution, 38, 40
  industrial devastation in, 31
  inflation in, 24, 25, 26, 27
  manufacturing investment in, 38, 39
  manufacturing output in, 22–23, 25,
    29, 33
  money supply growth rate, 35
  patents in, 46

Great Britain *(continued)*
  productivity growth in, 5, 6
  unemployment in, 23–24, 26, 29, 30,
    32–34

H

Hahn, Frank, 32
Harrod, R., 67
Hong Kong, 157–58

I

Income distribution, 75, 91, 112–13
  in Great Britain, 38, 40
Industrial supplies, 124
Inflation, 112, 114, 133, 167, 173, 177
  and austerity measures, 116
  and exchange rates, 73–74
  and full employment, 137–46
  in Great Britain, 24, 25, 26, 27
  and interest rates, 80–81, 131
  and money growth, 28–31
  and savings, 159–60, 163
  theories of, 163
  and unemployment, 109, 130–31,
    139–40
Infrastructure investment, 122
Innovation. *See* Technology
Interest rates
  and inflation, 80–81, 131
  manipulation of, 59
  and transactions demand, 110
International trade. *See* Trade
Investment, 157, 168–70
  and aggregate demand, 120–21, 130
  and automation, 175
  and balance of trade, 75
  composition of, 121, 122
  and consumption, 122
  crowding-in effect, 161
  in Great Britain, 19
  intra-triad foreign direct, 55
  Japanese foreign direct, 54
  in manufacturing, 38, 39

Investment *(continued)*
and NAFTA, 65–66
policies, 134
and productivity growth slowdown,
112
public, 122, 161, 165, 171
and transactions demand, 110

J

Japan, 14–15, 45, 63, 77, 174, 176
foreign direct investment by, 54
patents in, 46
productivity growth in, 5

K

Kaldor, Nicholas, 48, 133
Keynes, John Maynard, 12, 139
Keynesianism, 177–78
Korea, 78, 158–59

L

Labor
demand growth, 102, 104
growth rates of hours, 83
markets, 142
payments and costs, 152–56
productivity, 43, 48–49
and employment, 147
growth, 149
supply growth, 102–03, 104
unions, 107
unit costs, 70–72, 77
unskilled, 79–82
capital good substitution for, 82
cost of, 80–82
and policy, 84–85
See also Employment;
Unemployment; Wages
Labor-saving process innovations, 42,
53
Law of Correlated Prices (LCP),
69–70, 71

Law of One Price (LOP), 69
Lawson, Nigel, 22
LCP. *See* Law of Correlated Prices
Leontief, W., 69
Licensing, 52
Living standards, 93–94
Lloyd, Selwyn, 22–23
LOP. *See* Law of One Price
Luddites, 152–53

M

Maastricht Treaty, 18
Maddison, Angus, 43, 46
Manufacturing, 5–6, 38, 39
Marshall-Lerner-Robinson-Metzler
elasticities problem, 68
Mass production, 109
McCloskey, D.N., 70
Mechanization, 83–84
Mexico, 65–66, 77
MFA. *See* Multifiber Arrangement
Military service, 120
Minimum wage, 107
Modernization, 75–76
Monetarism, 27–28, 110, 163
Monetary policy, 139, 140, 141, 142,
145
Monetary system, 110
Money. *See* Currency; Exchange
rates
Money supply, 110
Monopoly rents, 42
Multifiber Arrangement (MFA),
85
Multinational firms, 54–56

N

NAFTA. *See* North American Free
Trade Agreement
Natural rate theory, 140–41, 143
Neild, Robert, 32
Netherlands, 46
Nondurables, 119, 124

North American Free Trade Agreement
(NAFTA), 65–66, 77, 85
North Sea oil, 26

O

Oil, 26, 131
Oil shock, 131
Okun's law, 144–45
Output growth, 102–05

P

Participation rates, 151–52
Patents, 46, 54–55
Phelps, Edmund, 140
Phillips curve, 139–40, 143–45
Porter, Michael, 57
Poverty, 113
PPP. *See* Purchasing Power Parity
Price(s)
  adjustments, 142
  and international competition, 69–
    70
  levels, 62
  mechanism, 109–10
*Principles of Political Economy and
  Taxation* (Ricardo), 152
Product cycle trade theory, 44–45
Production conditions, 68–69
Productivity
  convergence, 45
  and international trade, 75–76
  labor, 43, 48–49, 147, 149
  See also Productivity growth
Productivity growth, 112–13
  and aggregate demand, 130–31
  and demand saturation, 151
  inducing, 157–59
  labor, 149
  manufacturing, 5–6
  and market interventions, 148
  and technology, 5–7
  and unskilled labor, 80, 83
  U.S., 5, 46–47, 88–90

Productivity growth *(continued)*
  and wage growth, 100–102, 104–07,
    112–13, 154–55
Product life cycles, 42, 51–52
Profit-led economies, 155
Protectionism, 59, 75, 85, 160
Protopapadakis, A.A., 70
Purchasing Power Parity (PPP), 62,
  74

Q

Quotas, 160

R

Regulating producers, 70–71
Republican policies, 114–16
Research and development, 57, 58
  cost of, 52
  internationalization of, 52–53, 54–55
  by multinational firms, 55
Ricardo, David, 67, 152–53

S

Savings, 159–60
Second-order industries, 175
Semiconductors, 43–44
Services, 118–19, 124, 130, 150
Sharp, M., 56
Smith, Adam, 66–67
Sociopolitical premises, 177
Speculation, 10–12, 116
Stol, H.R., 70
Structuralism, 163
Summers, Lawrence, 80

T

Taiwan, 77, 158–59
Tanzania, 161
Taxation, 146
  and aggregate demand, 125–26
  in Great Britain, 31

Technology, 5–7, 174–76
  American leadership in, 43–47
  convergence and competition in,
      47–51, 57–58
  diffusion of, 41, 50, 176
  and competition, 51–54
  rates of, 54–56
  and strategic alliances, 56–57
  and employment growth, 41–43
  and international performance
      differences, 177
  and international trade, 69
  keeping up versus catching up, 49–51
  labor-saving process, 42, 53
  rates of return for, 42
  and white-collar unemployment, 53
Thatcher, Margaret, 21–22, 26
Trade, 7–8
  and aggregate demand, 123–24
  alternate approach to theory of,
      66–76
  conventional analyses of, 60–65
  free trade, 59–77
  and exchange rates, 61–62
  imbalances, 15
  impact of theory on policy, 65–66
  product cycle theory, 44–45
  rise in, 131–32
Training programs, 85
Transactions demand, 110
Transfer costs, 69
Transfer payments, 128

U

Underemployment, 90–91, 94,
    111
Unemployment, 173
  average annual civilian, 94
  average duration of, 143–44
  and declining wages, 88–100
  and earnings potential, 97, 99
  equilibrium rate of, 143
  and free trade, 59–77

Unemployment *(continued)*
  in Great Britain, 23–24, 26, 29, 30,
      32–34, 37, 38
  and inflation, 109, 130–31
  and international financial
      environment, 8–14
  and international structural change,
      7–8
  and macroeconomic policy, 27–28
  natural level of, 110, 140–41
  postwar periods in, 111–12
  skilled rate of, 79
  and technological change, 5–7
  and technological competition, 41–58
  unskilled, 79–85
  and wage growth, 100–108
  white-collar, 53, 58
  of women, 112
  on world scale, 3–20
  See also Employment; Full
      employment
United Kingdom. See Great Britain
United States, 17, 63, 110, 176
  aggregate demand in, 109–35
  austerity measures in, 116
  black unemployment in, 79
  and Bretton Woods system, 14
  economic decline of, 41, 46–47,
      173–74
  economic theory in, 177–80
  employment in, 13
  growth rates in, 103–04
  innovation in, 42
  multinational firms in, 54, 55
  and NAFTA, 65–66, 76
  patents in, 46
  productivity growth in, 5, 46–47
  Democratic vs. Republican policies
      and, 113–16
  technological leadership of, 43–47
  trade imbalances, 15
  unemployment, 114, 137–38, 173
  average annual civilian, 94
  wages in, 87–108, 173

United States *(continued)*
white-collar unemployment in, 53
Unit labor costs, 70–71, 77
and exchange rates, 72
Universal military service, 120
Universities, 84

V

Vernon, Raymond, 44

W

Wage-led economies, 155, 160
Wages, 173
and aggregate demand, 153–55, 160
growth, 152–56
alternate paths for, 102–03
and productivity growth, 100–102,
112–13, 154–55
and right-wing policies, 104–05
and unemployment, 99, 100–108
and incomes policies, 134
and interest rates, 80–81
and international trade, 68–69, 72
low wage competition, 8
minimum, 107

Wages *(continued)*
and technological convergence, 50
in United States, 87–108
decline in, 87–88
future of, 105–08
growth in, 104
hours worked per capita, 92, 93
median family income, 93–94
potential, 90–100
real spendable hourly earnings,
91–93, 98, 99–100
Wage-threshold scheme, 26
War on Poverty, 120
Welfare dependency, 85
White-collar unemployment, 53, 58
Women, 112
Workers' employment earnings
potential, 90–100

X

Xerox Corporation, 56

Z

Zecher, J.R., 70
Zimbabwe, 161

————— Contributors —————

Alice H. Amsden is the Ellen Swallow Richards Professor of Political Economy at the Massachusetts Institute of Technology, and former Professor of Economics at the New School for Social Research. She is the author of *Asia's Next Giant* (1989) and a co-author of *The Market Meets its Match: Restructuring the Economies of Eastern Europe* (1994).

John Eatwell is a Fellow of Trinity College, Cambridge, and a Professor at the New School for Social Research, New York. He was a co-editor of *The New Palgrave Dictionary of Economics* (1987) and *The New Palgrave Dictionary of Money and Finance* (1992). He has recently co-authored a study of transition policies in eastern Europe entitled *Transformation and Integration* (1995).

David M. Gordon is Dorothy H. Hirshon Professor of Economics and Director of the Center of Economic Policy Analysis at the New School for Social Research. He is author of *Fat and Mean: How Bloated Corporate Management and Falling Wages Squeeze Working Americans and Shackle our Economy* (1996).

Wynne Godley is a Fellow of King's College, Cambridge, and was until recently Director of the Department of Applied Economics at Cambridge University. He is a Senior Fellow at the Jerome Levy Economics Institute of Bard College. He is a member of the panel of independent economic advisors to the British Chancellor of the Exchequer.

Robert Heilbroner is Norman Thomas Professor (emeritus) at the New School for Social Research. He is the author of numerous books, most recently *Visions of the Future* (1995), and (with William Millberg) *The Crisis of Vision in Modern Economic Thought* (1996).

Edward J. Nell is Malcolm B. Smith Professor of Economics at the New School for Social Research. He is the author of *Prosperity and Public Spending* (1988), *Transformational Growth and Effective Demand* (1992), and the forthcoming *Making Sense of a Changing Economy*.

Thomas Palley is a Professor at the New School for Social Research. He specializes in monetary macroeconomics. He has recently published "Competing views of the money supply" in *Metroeconomica*, and "Debt, aggregate demand, and the business cycle" in the *Journal of Post-Kenesian Economics*.

David Schwartzman is a Professor of Economics at the New School for Social Research. He is the author of *The Japanese Television Cartel: A Study based on Matsushita v. Zenith*. He is working on a study of black and unskilled unemployment.

Anwar Shaikh is Professor of Economics at the New School for Social Research. His research and publications cover production theory, distribution theory, Marxian theory, international trade, nonlinear dynamics, the welfare state and the social wage, long-term growth and technical change, exchange rates, and, more recently, the dynamics of the U.S. stock market. He is a co-author of *Measuring the Wealth of Nations: The Political Economy of National Accounts* (1994).

Lance Taylor is Arnhold Professor of Economics at the New School for Social Research. His work focuses on the macroeconomic and environmental aspects of stabilization and adjustment in developing and post-socialist countries. He is the author of *Income Distribution, Inflation and Growth* (1991), and co-author of *The Market Meets its Match: Restructuring the Economies of Eastern Europe* (1994).

DATE DUE

~~OCT 2 3 1997~~		
~~DEC 1 5 1997~~		
~~MAY 1 2 1998~~		
~~JUN 0 4 1998~~		
~~JUN 2 9 2000~~		
~~NOV 2 9 2003~~		
		Printed in USA